To Luciana, Gianpaolo, Vivara, Priscilla

natural energy

gino finizio**architecture&mobility**

tradition and innovation

organisation

Cover
The Fiat factory at the Lingotto,
view of the internal ramp
(photo FIAT, graphic editing by Gino Finizio)

On page 2
Dinos

On page 5
ark.mob, *Digital Collage from Piet Mondrian*
(graphic editing endstart)

Cover Design
Marcello Francone

Design
endstart

Editing
Mary Rooney

Layout
Philippe Casens

Translation
Leslie Ray, Language Consulting
Congressi, Milan

First published in Italy in 2006 by
Skira Editore S.p.A.
Palazzo Casati Stampa
via Torino 61
20123 Milano
Italy
www.skira.net

Printed and bound in Italy. First edition

ISBN-13: 978-8861-30-071-2
ISBN-10: 88-6130-071-5

Distributed in North America by Rizzoli International Publications, Inc.,
300 Park Avenue South, New York, NY 10010.
Distributed elsewhere in the world by Thames and Hudson Ltd.,

Materials and research
John Bennett
John Blanchard
Eduard Böhtlingk
Efrem Bonacina
Chiara Buoncristiani
Silvia Clemente
Emanuele Corcagnani
Paolo Corcagnani
Jan De Kok
Roberto Delfanti
Lorenzo Facchini
Vivara Finizio
Francesco Fittipaldi
Andy Flenzel
Claudio Formicola
Luigi Formicola
Margherita Franco
Marc García Rojals
Rosalinda Iuliano
Diego Marinelli
Francesco Paretti
Marcello Sebis
Mauro Tedeschini
Edoardo Terrone
Alessandro Villa

Contributions
Tadao Ando
Ron Arad
Mario Bellini
Lucius Burckhardt
Antonio Citterio
Nigel Coates
Coop Himmelb(l)au
Riccardo Dalisi
Michele De Lucchi
Norman Foster
Massimiliano Fuksas
Frank O. Gehry
Giorgetto Giugiaro
Zaha Hadid
Isao Hosoe
Toshiyuki Kita
Rem Koolhaas
Alessandro Mendini
Jean Nouvel
Pietro Palladino
Renzo Piano
Richard Sapper
Fred Scott
Richard Serra
Philippe Starck

Thanks
Daniela Aleggiani
Mario Botta
Pietro Camardella
Nevio Di Giusto
Gillo Dorfles
Ignazia Favata
Mario Galfetti
Miguelangel Galluzzi
Alfonso Gambardella
Virginia Gangeni
Roberto Giolito
Maria Grazia Mazzocchi
Mauro Porcini
Rodrigo Rodriquez
Piercipriano Rollo
Sante Terrone

Photographs
Enrico Cano
Rodolfo Facchini
endstart Gianpaolo Finizio
Stefano Goldbergh
Jean-Baptiste Mondino
Sanne Pepper
Zaha Hadid Architects

Contents

Part 3:   Applications – Transportation Design, Design

Preface

Gillo Dorfles

Even if it is easy to imagine—as science fiction—an age not far in the future when people will move around in futuristic metropolises using tiny airborne vehicles, probably based on some anti-gravitational system, I nevertheless believe that at least a few decades will have to go by before the car as we know it ceases to be the main means of transport for our social lives. For this reason, this new text by Gino Finizio on the theme of 'forms in movement' can be considered as a versatile yet densely packed compendium of all the most up-to-date hypotheses regarding the present and future of the relationship between 'static architecture' and 'dynamic architecture' today, which is in fact that of the car if considered in relation to the most advanced architecture of our times. Finizio has not only presented some of his most original ideas regarding the current state of architecture and design (and especially car design) in this volume, but he has also called upon some of the most committed architect-designers to report on their research. This is not only 'conceptual', but has also been conducted by the authors themselves at certain important research centres, professional studios and universities, together with Finizio himself and with the involvement of numerous students, in order to perfect certain new, and often entirely unprecedented, designs relating to the world of the car. Of course, the projects presented in this book, the result of previous work and detailed presentations by the individual authors concerned, are to a large extent the result of the initiative associated with the Fiat Research Centre, coordinated by Studio Gino Finizio Design & Management, which is to undergo further analyses and technical examination. Yet, as of now, the projects enable us to realise that many issues exist, today feasible, which concentrate on questions that are all too often neglected by designers and by the companies present in this sector. Before dealing specifically with the crucial issues of the car, it seems to me to be appropriate to first say a few words on the current situation of our cities and their relationship with traffic and with citizens' mobility. This is what Finizio says in this regard: 'Cities appear to be governed by chaos… The city is accepted as pure coexistence of objects without visual or formal relationships, released from architectural connections. The city is understood no longer as a fabric, but as mere coexistence'. As can be seen, from the very beginning, the very concept of city and metropolis abounds with ambiguities: the continuous uncoordinated development of anonymous suburbs, the move towards ever larger conurbations housing more than 50% of the planet's population, these are a sore point destined to become gangrenous if a remedy is not soon found to the problem of traffic and a return to the countryside is not encouraged. In fact this is already practicable today, above all because of the presence of many freelance jobs—which are literally 'home-based'—made possible by the new means of communication using I.T. However, as of now, taking a look at the situation of the most advanced architecture, we can recognise certain essential elements that have been highlighted by the various experts consulted by the author. For instance, according to Alessandro Mendini, there is an 'absence of rituality' in the modern city, while urban design: 'should attempt to connect to previous cultures, whereas urban furnishing must present itself as set designing.' Or else, according to Gehry, architecture can be described as a 'metaphor of movement' 'in the energy emitted from daring, light forms, which hover weightlessly' and that, according to Finizio 'are comparable to those of

10

means of transport, of cars, of fast trains. It is evident that Gehry's metal surfaces transmit above all a sense of liberty'. Even if, in this case, the reference to the well known building in Prague (the Nationale Nederlanden) is not among the most effective, there is no doubt that many of the architect's constructions recall the design of a non-static mobile object. But perhaps it is Fuksas' city that, albeit in its visionary aspect, appears closer to an existing, amendable reality. 'Fuksas' city—Finizio affirms—admits disorder as a natural form of "sublime" order (we have recent evidence of this in the imposing realisation for the new Milan Fair).' 'What has always fascinated me is the beauty of the absence of form—says Fuksas—the imperfection of beauty'. It is impossible for me to cite all the opinions offered by the architects consulted by Finizio, such as Lucius Burckhardt, Rem Koolhaas, Jean Nouvel, Alessandro Mendini, etc. The fact is symptomatic, however, that, even before attempting a new design approach to the car, almost all of them have admitted that the urban planning crisis—more than the specifically architectural on—prevents any sure solution, at least for now. If at this point, after the indispensable urbanistic-architectural introductory statements, we wish to face what constitutes the true theme of the essay, that is, what model of a truly innovative car can be hypothesised, we will see that the various formulations of the problem, by Bellini, Citterio, Dalisi, De Lucchi, Hosoe, Mendini, Nouvel, Sapper and Kita, are actually all very different from each other. Starting from the existing and in many ways innovative model by Smart, it will appear obvious that the problems of spatial limitation, comfort and respect for ecology are among the first and dominant requirements in almost all the research conducted. However, so as not to dwell on the most meaningful examples, I would immediately like to cite the two most charming: that of the 'car-slipper' by Dalisi and that by Michele De Lucchi, 'Small'. While the former—based on a Fiat 127 chassis—has developed a futuristic type of small car, not fast, but very 'domestic', fitted with a rain canopy, of a considerable height, a central door, a folding double bonnet, etc., the second envisages the minimum possible dimensions, a monovolumetric (anti-rounding) pyramid form and a very thick platform, containing the whole engine part of the car. The projects by Bellini (where the dashboard is the central control unit, while information involves not only the driver but also the other 'passengers') are also certainly of considerable interest; as is that by Isao Hosoe, for whom 'the car becomes a small one-room flat that can move from the home' and where comfort is not only studied ergonomically but based on the user's perceptive and anthropometric aspects. It is not possible for me to dwell further on the individual peculiarities of these interesting projects; however, they do all demonstrate that 'fashion' alone is not enough to even out forms and impose a 'style' that often does not have a true raison d'être. The example of the 'Japanese-style' ovoid car, which for so long has imposed a certain taste on so many European cars, would be sufficient. If now, at the end of this brief and incomplete review of the various projects, we ask ourselves which of them will be able to meet with the most widespread approval and offer a real solution to the highly intricate problem of traffic and the very survival of our cities—provided we do not give up or seek consolation in hypotheses from science fiction (as I said at the start)—, I believe the only real answer for a (near) future of the car can be that of its 'sizing' and, at the same time, that of the elimination of pollution. Perhaps a 'mini-automobile', which is at the same time more comfortable, more ecological, more diversified, more personalised, more computerised, can allow—for a few decades at least—the survival of this prodigious—and apparently irreplaceable—'self-propelled symbol' of our age.

11

Preface

Alfonso Gambardella

When, at the beginning of the last century, Marinetti and the theorists of Futurism grasped a fundamental aspect of progress associated with temporal acceleration, the car took its first steps.

Only a few realised how much this tool would revolutionise the appearance of cities in the future. Few intellectuals understood the importance such an invention would take on in the economy of nations. In just a few decades, mobility would become absolutely revolutionary and the configuration of cities would be powerfully conditioned by it.

In the same period, the Modern movement was born, while the academies, though still developing theories associated with the tradition of the final years of the 19th century, entered a phase of quiescence. Technological innovation had already given birth to new means of transport: cars, planes and ships, striking the imaginations of great architects who were inspired by the theme of mobility, taking up formal and functional suggestions from the repertoire of locomotive systems to shape the new architecture.

We need only think of Le Corbusier and his explicit references to naval architecture, to the materials and techniques used for cars, trains and planes. Slowly the new architectural functionalism changed the overall image of the city, while a new technological vision imposed new models even in the selection of the project options.

A further stimulus for the imagination and creativity appears to have been the relationship that associated the idea of a new architecture with the myth of technological progress, in the hope of being able to draw on a wide range of expressive potentials, connected with the futuristic world of means of transport.

Many images by the architects of Expressionism, above all utopian visions, denounce the aspiring to a glorious architecture that copies the dynamism and forms of planes and spaceships. On this subject, we would like to mention the designs of Wenzel A. Hablik, including the flying neighbourhood in orbit for a year, made of metal and valuable glass, the glass and reinforced concrete house submerged in the sea, which is lowered in the event of storms, as it has the characteristics of a thermal island, and the city-district for explorers, the forerunner of the current space shuttles: a metal sphere, suspended, light as aluminium, hard as steel, transparent as glass.

Today the imitative relationship, which in the Modern movement clearly linked the theme of architecture with the theme of mobility, seems to have changed tack and to be proceeding in the opposite direction compared with the past. The most evident signs of this are recognisable in the most recent car designs.

Indeed, it is no longer the house that becomes more similar every day to the car, in the name of extreme dynamism, of movement, both physical and conceptual, but rather it is the car that becomes increasingly like a house, abandoning the myth of speed, to seek above all inhabitability, the comfort of the interior, reconciliation with urban spaces, with the structure of the old historic centres, respecting ecological equilibria, energy saving, the elimination of environmental pollution.

A car that is liveable and flexible, to suit the most diverse and sudden needs that are revealed; a car whose character as 'mobile architecture' is prevalent over the idea of fast cars in eternal movement.

Gino Finizio's research fits within this framework; he shows skill and sensitivity in dealing with a problem, the imagining of innovative scenarios for the designing of cars, of which he has long been an attentive observer and promoter of strategies, contacts, hybridisations, capable of stimulating and accelerating processes of radical and culturally advanced transformation in the automobile sector.

This text is among the most significant testimonies of the goals already reached in the process of innovation undertaken by car manufacturing companies, and of the perspectives already specifically delineated, revealing glimpses of what the future of this means of locomotion will be, in a society where elements are increasingly emerging of diversity of a cultural, social, religious, ethnic and geographical character, which will probably require a closer connection between the designing of the means of transport and the demands of individual locations.

The collaboration of prestigious designers who have long been committed to the theme of mobility, as documented extensively in this volume, offers a further guarantee of an organic development of the research conducted by Gino Finizio to date, with more than gratifying results.

Introduction

The car is the industrial product that has most influenced society and contributed most to improving personal mobility. Its diffusion has grown to the point of being considered a possession that is necessary for families and individuals, synonymous with liberty and autonomy of movement.

Traffic congestion in the most densely populated areas has seriously challenged this prerogative.

Due to the evils of the city, pollution first and foremost, the car has changed from being a symbol of well-being. This is an urgent problem, which prompts us to revise the concept of mobility as a whole and to extend our horizons of research from the vehicle to the road system, from the architecture of the car to its relationship with architecture. To go down this path, it is necessary to analyse and recognise the aspects that emerge from the industrial history of the car that are worth preserving, in order to consolidate them.

At the same time, it is important to favour possible evolutions, in order to make the car match the times we are living in, meet people's real needs, and to make this industrial architecture in movement an object that participates in the existing and future urban landscape.

This volume analyses two interrelated themes:
• *Architecture and mobility*
• *Tradition and innovation*

In other words, we have identified what the possible integration between architecture and mobility should be, in the sense of the reciprocal interface, in terms of an efficient and minimal relationship of scale, technology in favour of ecology, of the environment, of people. The chameleon-car is a vehicle concept that is suited to all environments, from the city street to the open country road, and satisfies the requisite that makes it desirable, the freedom to choose routes. It is a versatile car that has developed a form of intelligence capable of responding to the obstacles it encounters. Steady-car is a microenvironment that establishes a dialogue with the existing central and peripheral architectures, also positioning itself as an extension of these, and thus a specialised and flexible environment to aid domestic inhabitability, becoming less and less an element of disruption for the urban landscape. The designing of new forms of mobility cannot be disregarded when imagining a new conception of a road network, to envisage differentiated solutions in relation to the context. It is indispensable to design intelligent cars for intelligent roads if we are to improve the peripheral road systems. It is indispensable for cars to be able to enter city centres, whether historical or recently built, in a less aggressive and invasive way, favouring, for example, the passage from a form of possession to a mode of access. It is also necessary to pay attention to the new forms of organisation of the territory, to replace the traditional centre-periphery dichotomy. This book is intended to stimulate design engineers, urban planners, architects, designers and managers of services to envisage a common language, a form of artificial intelligence that accomplishes a visible integration between static volumes and forms in movement.

LOCUS PAESAGGIO CAOS ⊥ LE CORBUSIER) MATERIA
URBANO CAOS ⊥ TTORI CAOS ↓ STERN)
BURCKHARDT CAOS ← CAOS CAOS NOUVELL
← ⊥ CAOS REM KOOLHAAS ∫
CAOS CAOS
QUALE PAESAGGIO URBANO) TRASPARENZA

FRANK O. GEHRY) MICHELE.
DE LUCCHI
SCENOGRAFIA ⊂ NUOVE PEPSI ⏋ ARIA
BILBAO ⌐ CITTÀ ⊂
→ ALESSANDRO MENDINI MASSIMILIANO
NAPOLI RINASCE ⊤ ARTE (FUKSAS)
DALISI CIABATTA ⊤ ⌐ LA CITTÀ DEL
RICIRARD NUOVA) FUORI DAL FUTURO
⌐ CULTURA ↓ CENTRO ⊂
PIENA
NON LUOGHI ⤬ MARIO BELLINI
ANTONIO IDESIGN NIGEL COATES ⊥ ( ) L'UOMO DEL FUTURO
CITTERIO SMATTI TRUCCO ⊂ PARIGI
↙ AUTOOGGETTO → AUTOSELVUO ⊂
ARREDARE DAO HOSSEIN KITATOSCHI KITA ∫
COD CULARE ← ⊥⤬ RETE VIRTUALE
RICHARD
BOLGARI SAPPER APPLE ↙ ↗ RENZO PIANO
(IBM) GENIO
ZAHA HADID GENIO DALL'ALTO DEL
PIETRO ⊂
DI LUCE PROPRIA PALLADINO LINGOTTO

Book Structure

This book is structured into three distinct parts; a thread running through the text highlights the relationship between *architecture and mobility*, the issues deriving from congestion in city centres, and proposes a planning commitment to identify a technologically advanced mobility in harmony with the environment.

Part 1: Scenario – Architecture and Mobility

This part studies the changes in the contemporary city, the urban landscape, the architectures of a different nature and language, the road network and its articulated development.

It investigates the possible transformation of means of transport, from private to public use, the influence of the virtual network as innovation that proposes new modes and systems for communication and the reduction of distances.

There follows an in-depth investigation that analyses the thought, projects and activities associated with the theme, by architects, designers and mobility experts such as Lucius Burckardt, Rem Koolhaas, Jean Nouvel, Michele De Lucchi, Frank O. Gehry, Alessandro Mendini, Massimiliano Fuksas, Antonio Citterio, Mario Bellini, Renzo Piano, Zaha Hadid, Pietro Palladino and Tadao Ando.

Part 2: State of the Art – Tradition and Innovation

History and the temptation of the new, revising the sense of construction and the size problem, the relationship between space and object, materials and technologies, people and territory.

There follows an in-depth investigation that analyses the thought, projects and activities associated with the theme, by architects, designers, experts on project culture, in addition to those already mentioned, such as Mario Botta, Nigel Coates, Giorgetto Giugiaro, Eduard Böhtlingk, Mecanoo, Norman Foster, Coop Himmelb(l)au, Achille Castiglioni, Ross Lovegrove, Ron Arad, Joe Colombo and Fred Scott.

Part 3: Applications – Transportation Design, Design

This part concerns the design of means and systems of transport viewed from a very broad perspective that envisages intelligent vehicles that communicate with each other and interface with the territory. It also shows the design concepts for cars developed by the masters of design and top industrial executives, in addition to those already mentioned, such as Riccardo Dalisi, Isao Hosoe, Richard Sapper, Toshiyuki Kita, Ermanno Cressoni, Nevio di Giusto, Roberto Giolito and Pietro Camardella.

1 Architecture^Mobility

1.1

Which Urban Landscape?

The speed and complexity of the altering of the urban landscape make the interpretation of change using the traditional critical instruments difficult. Architects and experts emphasise the inadequacy of the conventional notion of planning in governing the development of the city (Koolhaas, Nouvel, De Lucchi, Gehry, Mendini, Fuksas, Citterio, Bellini, Piano, Hadid, Burkhardt). From their contributions the image emerges of the contemporary city: generic, diffuse, generated by the coexistence of differing, apparently irreconcilable structures.

1.2

Outside the Centre

In the diffuse metropolis, does a centre still exist? The extension of *metropolitan* characteristics to the territory transforms the city from a territorial entity into a qualitative category, with effects on the forms of movement. Many architects and experts are therefore prompted to interpret the urban structure according to a logic that transcends the traditional distinction between centre and periphery.

1.3

The Road Network

The road network is extensive and makes large parts of our planet accessible. The need for mobility in developing countries prompts us to consider the characteristics of total interdependence of the vehicle/road system. The problems of excessive congestion associated with the mobility of industrialised countries lead us to reflect on the need to develop an evolved relationship between roads and architecture.

1.4

From Car-as-object to Car-as-service

The limited effectiveness of public transport in resolving traffic problems makes it necessary to identify new ways of conceiving the car. The 'car-as-service', designed to respond dynamically to changing conditions and individual tastes, is the true rival of the current 'car-as-object', or product, and suggests an alternative scenario of mobility to the current dichotomy that sees public and private means of transport in opposition to each other.

1.5

The Virtual Network

Virtual space is not yet a genuine rival to the real and physical mobility of people, but it is a network in which vehicles will move at the same time and as an alternative to real movements. Real advantages in the management of traffic on the road network may result from the ability to connect the vehicle up to the virtual network.

1.1

Which Urban Landscape?

The urban landscape changes. The speed of these changes makes interpreting them and any possibility of forecasting them difficult. The best architects give the issue a great deal of consideration and attempt to anticipate the results of changes, to prevent them from being merely the result of chance and economic mechanisms. The traditional urban planning tools have proven to be inadequate when faced with the complexity of processes.

Cities appear to be governed by chaos and many theories propose the awareness and acceptance of 'dis-order', as a necessary condition for understanding the complexity of transformations.

It follows that the traditional notion of the plan appears inadequate when it comes to governing development.

The planning scheme, constructed starting from a 'topographical' reading of the context, positions itself as a programme of strategies and performance, avoiding taking shape as a plan on compositional bases, which would inevitably be disregarded with changing economic and political conditions.

The loss of faith in ideologies and the difficulty in laying a theoretical basis for the processes of transformation of the city have favoured the development of new ways of interpreting the urban context. The city is accepted as pure coexistence of objects without visual or formal relations, released from architectural connections.

Judgement has been suspended on the city composed of a mass of mediocre buildings, yet this does not prevent us from sometimes appreciating its spectacular aspects. The suspension of judgement is claimed to be the only condition for being able to intervene with projects in desperate urban situations.

Freeing ourselves from preconceptions enables us to implement experimentation as method, the limits of which are set by the very conditions of the project. The effects of the processes of transformation of 'metropolises' are also reflected in the perception of the landscape in general. As Lucius Burckhardt underlines, the medium of perception of this landscape, more or less urbanised, is represented by the route visitors must follow to reach the buildings and forms of architecture that interest them. The same applies for the venue of activities.

Land abandoned by agriculture and industry, car parks, enormous empty areas, motorway intersections or waste disposal sites; these are all continually growing residual surfaces that characterise the metropolis. Burckhardt cites the case of the modern town hall, which is no longer located in the square of the same name and needs to communicate its presence exclusively through the means of architecture.

There results a proliferation of pretentious approved buildings, which are not very accessible from the exterior: 'cactuses in the desert of the anti-city'. In practice, we feel the absence of that route/walk that in the traditional city gradually takes us to objects and places. A route filled with information on what awaits us, which does not preclude a sense of surprise when faced with the architectural construction, but which frees the building from the need to stake a claim to its own presence and function in the territory with inadequate instruments. Yet the new forms of urbanisation do not seem capable of creating significant new routes to approach architecture, not even for use solely by vehicle traffic.

Rem Koolhaas is certainly the architect who has identified and described the changes in the contemporary city most lucidly and insightfully.

Since the 1990s, the famous Dutch architect has distinguished and established himself on the international scene by a new way of interpreting and taking action in the city, now no longer understood as a fabric, but as a *mere* coexistence, a place of relations between objects that are almost never articulated visually or formally, no longer *captured* by architectural connections.

But if we arrive at the conclusion that connection is no longer necessary—as Koolhaas himself warns us—then the bases of the discipline and the profession are placed in doubt.

Therefore, in short, what has supposedly killed urban planning is not the fact that desperate errors have been committed on many occasions, but the fact that very few of the processes and operations under way today can be translated into the form of a plan, the classic instrument of urban planning.

The crisis in urban planning puts the planner in the position of depending on the existing conditions, with respect to which he must measure himself with his own personal judgement, partly intuitive, partly explicit, as his sole guide as to where the potential space for that interpretation that generates the project is identified.

And it is on this judgement that the representation of the system, positive or negative, neutral or impassioned, depends. An architect, and a remarkable graphic artist, Rem Koolhaas suggests imposing on conceptually evolved architectures, an architectural vision that makes us imagine a possible future in which the architecture favours mobility and communication.

The relationship between ancient and modern, *tradition and innovation*, is certainly complex and requires a serious commitment on the part of planners interested in the problem of new constructions, or in rebuilding old structures. The historical cities afflicted by vehicle traffic are a reality to which a precise and authoritative response must be given. A synthesis between *architecture and mobility* from the perspective described in this book is realised with this connection envisaged by Rem Koolhaas, who seems to be one of the major promoters of an order from chaos, in the sense that it is an integration between means of transport and place that receives and allows a greater functionality within the whole road system.

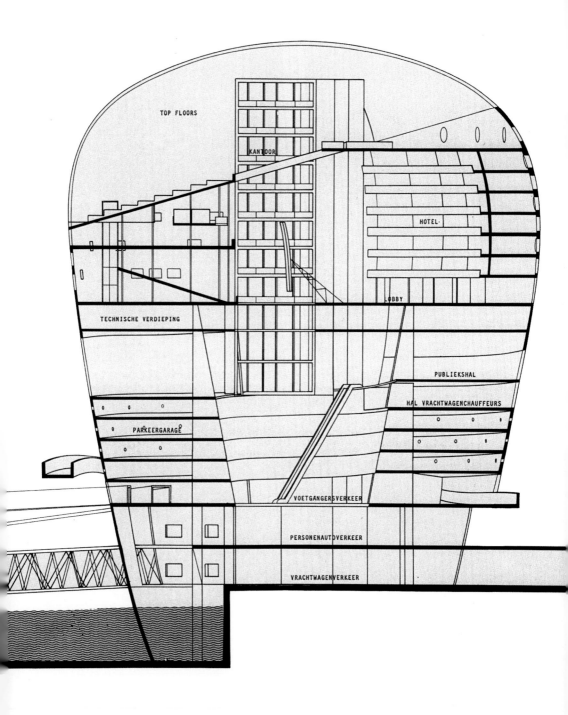

TOP FLOORS

KANTOOR

HOTEL·

LOBBY

TECHNISCHE VERDIEPING

PUBLIEKSHAL

HAL VRACHTWAGENCHAUFFEURS

PARKEERGARAGE

VOETGANGERSVERKEER

PERSONENAUTOVERKEER

VRACHTWAGENVERKEER

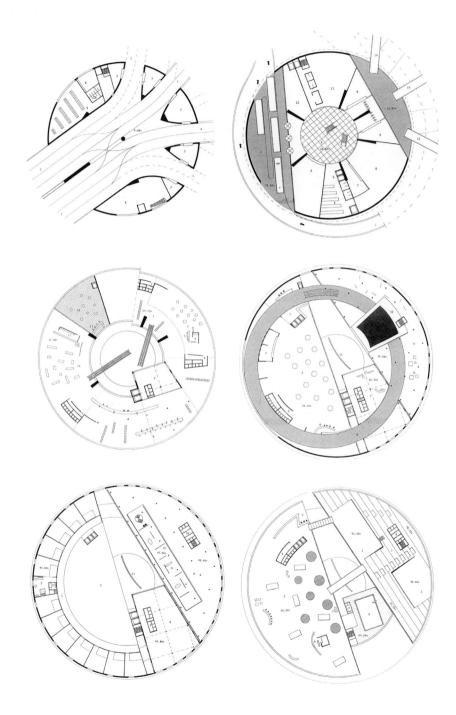

Rem Koolhaas

'City: the sketches cannot hide the fact that most of the supporters of urban super-highways do not love cities very much.
Almost all the initial supporters of super-highways were equally convinced that cities would disappear, that, thanks to decentralised roads, they would evolve towards a suburban, pastoral ideal, or that cities would be replaced by others conceived from different patterns.'

'Complexity: our model proposes to show certain properties of the evolution of complex systems and, in particular, the difficulty in governing a development determined between multiple elements that interact with each other.
What is quite clear is that the complexity of systems does not enable us to think following a linear causality or simple variables.'

¬ Rem Koolhaas, S, M, L, XL, *The Monacelli Press, Rotterdam 1995*

'My conclusion is that chaos is something intrinsically inaccessible to architects.
We cannot aspire to it, but we can only be its instrument....
The only relationship architects can establish with chaos is to join the ranks of those who oppose it, and to fail.
And it is only in failure, by chance, that chaos is produced.'

¬ Alejandro Zaera, 'Finding freedoms: conversation with Rem Koolhaas', El Croquis, 53, 1992, 6–31

nouvel

Jean Nouvel is one of the most highly appreciated architects of our time. His works influence planners and designers in every part of the world. The materials used for his works are always carefully selected to be artfully shaped and to achieve excellence of form, guaranteeing a functional and scenic result. The creativity, innate in the great architect, is unique; his projects are therefore always original and innovative, giving rise to new design tendencies. The first thought expressed by the master has not undergone conceptual changes over the course of his creative career path; intelligence intervenes to complete the project without compromises and genius does not hesitate to intervene to perfect it during the project, breathing the magical air of the location. The innovations obtained in this way constitute, on each occasion, unprecedented experiences and new lessons of architecture to be disseminated in the world of culture and work. Nouvel's projects represent a possible future; his works are ageless living bodies that vibrate, emanating the first sounds of a new architecture, where art gains the upper hand against the monotony of urban building with unique and exciting architectural works.

The French architect perceives and disseminates culture; he knows how to read in people's minds and hearts: this allows him to produce forms of architecture that become icons of new social movements, such as the Institut du Monde Arabe in Paris. The Cartier Foundation, which is located in a new generation Parisian building, is the emblem of how the appropriate use of materials is able to make the structure solid and light at the same time and give the inhabitant security and freedom. A new language of architecture where transparent materials replace conventional ones and blend with the metal supporting ones, forming a single volume, light and imposing, according to a style that has spread rapidly in the world of planning. The *Less* table, designed for Unifor, is an essential product, rendered solid by Jean Nouvel's capacity to 'sew' together the structural elements under the table top, making them imperceptible: this product also demonstrates his expertise in the world of industrial design.

In the lecture delivered on receiving his honorary degree in Industrial Design, awarded to him for his unquestionable ability by the Second University of Naples, he gave rise to a unique event of particular scientific content and superb scenic effect. Inside the Ceremony Room of the Reggia di Caserta, full of young students, authorities and ordinary people, all joined together in respectful silence, the great architect recited the values of his architecture: for the day the king of the Bourbon Palace was a French king, crowned to honour merit, acclaimed by the 'Neapolitan people'.

Whatever each person's profession, contact with cultural institutions is important, particularly with young people, who represent the future in any sphere. It is necessary to be educators of ourselves, continually updating ourselves, to then pass on our experiences to a public capable of continuing along the path trodden by the master. Jean Nouvel is a citizen of the world who lives on the work sites, the direct expressions of his project energy; he is a person who gives renown and a sense of eternity to the places that receive his works.

Our era is strongly characterised by the architecture of the French master, who imparts education and culture to the hurried people of the virtual age. Nouvel's works are reminiscent of bodies in movement and indicate the possible evolutions that means of transport must envisage in the immediate future, reinforcing the interaction between static and dynamic architecture.

'It is true that, a priori, I try not to venture into general truths.
When truth is formulated in a very clear way, it is transformed into generalisation.
My architectures do not represent an exceptional situation, but rather a series of specific
cases. They are serial. I can work on a heroic programme and on invisible aspects.
From an urban point of view, my architectures are nothing more than models.
The only thing that is repeated is the attitude that leads us to analyse every situation
in advance so as to understand what could be done on the basis of the parameters
supplied, which include not only the local context, but also the problems of our time.
And once this is realised, the rest is all there to be done.
We can then begin to discuss urbanistic theory, how the city can or must evolve.
I have said this in the past and I will repeat it: the city must not evolve beginning
from fixed-term planning or from preconceived ideas.'*

¬ Jean Nouvel, in C. Diaz Moreno, E. García Grinda, 'A conversation with Jean Nouvel',
El Croquis, 112–13, 2002, 6–25

According to Jean Nouvel, the city has become a burning issue and this (irreversible) situation also contains a certain dose of poetry, a hidden quality to be discovered and on which to work. The fact of recognising the intrinsically chaotic condition of urban development does not imply taking a position in favour or against this, but simply leads to the observation that the architect's work today exists in the absence of structures, in unpredictability, in the brutal comparison of typologies, in a disorder that we would never have imagined and that nevertheless exists. Each new project represents a concrete solution that is inserted into the urban context, seeking to understand its vocation, but above all it paves the way for possible new developments. Nouvel's thought avails itself of the experience accrued in the numerous projects that he has realised, or that are in the realisation phase, in many major cities. Projects that do not arise from the desire to represent a new paradigm of urban development, but come about as a pragmatic response, the result of a method that attributes great importance to the preliminary analysis as solid support, evidence, the necessary condition to give free rein to creativity, to the leap forward that is only fully realised in the project idea. According to Nouvel, there should be the possibility of changing one's mind at any moment in an urban project.

Development of the city must always take the present into consideration. Its future must, in fact, be constructed in relation to its past, as a result of the sum of many small gestures, guided by an inductive method and animated by the courage to propose creative solutions. The wisdom, the knowledge of the past, the capacity to live the contemporary world on a day-by-day basis make Jean Nouvel the architect who has been most capable, with the aid of suitable materials, of making volumes accessible, light and transparent, just as his sense of friendship is transparent.

Jean Nouvel and Gino Finizio, Reggia di Caserta, Palatine Chapel, 22 November 2002.

Michele De Lucchi

'I would like to say that the most beautiful and extraordinary material that exists, the most precious and rare, the most ductile, flexible and recyclable, is not plastic or aluminium, or some alloy of metals and resins, or the ultra-technological compound that nobody has invented yet, but is space, air; the air that we breathe and within which we walk, that we buy and sell and sculpt as though it were wax and that as long as it is there we do not worry, but that when it is missing we will not know where to go to get it, and we cannot produce it in a factory.

And then there is another material, also very expensive, which we never have now and we use very badly, and which—unfortunately—is not recyclable, and that is time, so very precious, the hours and days that we waste doing wrong and dangerous things, which are not just days and hours thrown away, but rather, days and hours spent doing ourselves harm.

Paradoxically, air and time are the least solid and tangible materials, but the ones that we waste most and that exist most on the earth in the form of qualities to be recovered, and not only in the form of material qualities, but also and above all sensory and spiritual qualities, if we can still talk of this.'

¬ Michele De Lucchi, January 1997

A designer's abilities are closely associated with his knowledge of the past and present and his capacity to imagine a possible future that proposes to innovate the existing without altering its acquired values. A good designer proposes variables, substitutions and creations that generate new concepts, systems and products increasingly suited to people and the environment. Often these are updates deriving from the appropriate use of innovative materials and new technologies, genuine inventions that revolutionise the system in use, fostering progress and modernity.

Michele De Lucchi is a true designer, a genuine revolutionary who creates innovation in the concepts that generate the products destined for the end market. Drawing strength from his experiences and his innate creative capacity, this well known architect breaks up obsolete systems to generate new energy that is spread with natural simplicity, realising the continuous process of *tradition and innovation*. Brand, image and communication, consistent with the company's mission and strategic positioning, are important factors for any industrial and service enterprise and, if correctly read by the market and by users, determine the real value of the company and its consequent success. Outstanding companies, in fact, become such precisely on account of the special care they devote over time to these factors, which become the driving force behind every business activity.

Michele De Lucchi knows these peculiar business disciplines well through direct experience and due to the profound sensibility he possesses as an industrial designer and architect; he has always developed his projects taking into major consideration these inspirations, which become decisive during the whole creative process. His contribution at the Triennial in Milan is a splendid project of architecture and interior design in a location deserving to be revisited by a contemporary master. The architect defines a design that gives spatiality, light, rigour, viability and beauty to the location, putting visitors at their ease in every environment. In the Triennial building in Milan people now circulate informed, free to see, to visit 'hands-on' the availability of art, transcending obsolete monumentalisms. Communication is the art of the century and the Triennial is the proper stage for it to perform its role. This is the case of Fiat Café, a space where you can admire the latest 'contaminations of design' that have penetrated the various market sectors.

Michele De Lucchi's sensibility for poetry, art, colour, services and ecology, can certainly favour—thanks to the vast echo of his projects—the integration between *architecture and mobility*, helping us emerge from the chaos that reigns in our tormented cities.

The project for the Poste Italiane, the Italian post office company, is a further clear demonstration of his expertise and concreteness in achieving the objectives previously set with the public services company distributed all over the country. The project for Poste Italiane has been developed and directed by Michele De Lucchi not only as an architecture project, but also as an updating of the entire system of mobility and functionality of the company's spaces and services. Having established the mission consistent with the company image, the new Italian post offices have been designed using contemporary and functional furnishing, appropriate for our times and capable of guaranteeing the physical and virtual mobility of all the services delivered in an efficient and safe way. The interior spaces have been designed to facilitate direct contact with the clientele, who now perceive the postal employee as a figure no longer 'hiding behind a counter' but as a staff member who helps, in real time, to satisfy the customer's demands. Open, colourful spaces that are uniform, comfortable and can be kept clean and tidy with easy maintenance. The ecological aspect, that is, the recycling of materials, and access for all, are always given due consideration. Availing himself of his business experience, Michele De Lucchi sustains that the new architecture of interiors for use by the public must communicate the company and its excellence. Through the integration between locations, means and systems, still and in movement, this architecture must lead to a perfect logistics that guarantees the complete efficiency of companies increasingly oriented towards customer satisfaction.

In conclusion, though the architectural project is developed autonomously and meticulously, it cannot be separated from a broader planning approach corresponding to the company's medium-term strategy and its positioning on the market of reference.

Frank O. Gehry

'Historically those who create three-dimensional objects attempt to capture the movement in forms.

Thus the statues of the Parthenon, like the dancing Shivas of India, that, if you look away and turn back, seem to have moved, have always fascinated me. I have studied with pure Modernists, for whom the past did not exist, so I was forced to replace it with an aesthetics that was significant for our time, something emotive, and I thought about "movement", the cars, aeroplanes, ships that attracted me through the movement they expressed.

Then came Postmodernism, with its obsessive revival of the past, which at the time I couldn't bear, and anyone who asked me about it received an ear-bashing that went on for hours. It seems to me to be absurd to have to look back. Was this really all we would be able to offer our children? Could it be possible that there was no way of expressing a contemporary ethics? To be polemical, I'm tempted to say: "If we have to go back to the Greeks, why not go back a further 300 million years to when there were only fish around?"

I built one for fun and I liked it a lot, then I made another more stylised one for an Italian fashion show at Palazzo Pitti, and it was a great success; they interviewed me about the fish. Later I started to think about fish as formal research, shiny, mobile surfaces; then I remembered the carps that my grandmother kept in the bathtub to make Gefilte and so I started to look for the instruments to describe those surfaces in a useful way.'

¬ Frank O. Gehry, 'Le mie architetture? Sono oniriche', interview, Il Manifesto, 29 October 2003

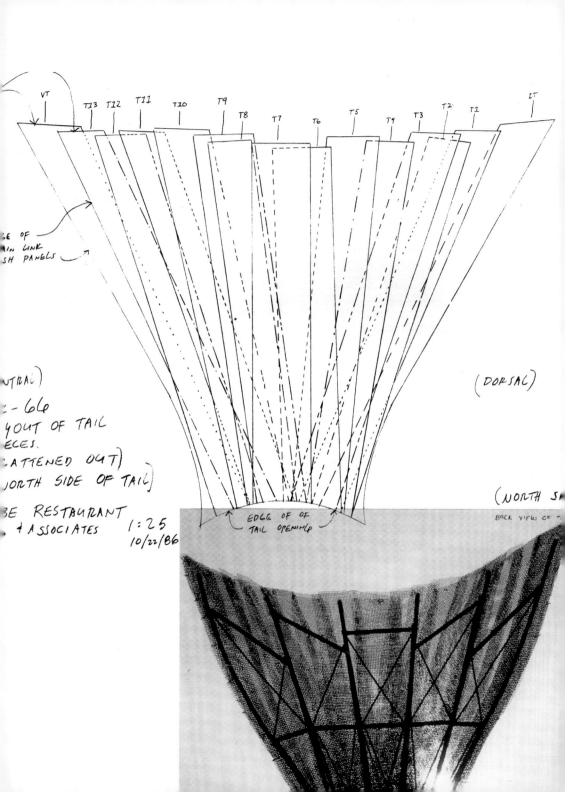

VT T13 T12 T11 T10 T9 T8 T7 T6 T5 T4 T3 T2 T1 LT

GE OF
AIN LINK
SH PANELS

(DORSAL)

TRAL)

:-66
YOUT OF TAIL
ECES.

ATTENED OUT)
ORTH SIDE OF TAIL)

BE RESTAURANT
+ ASSOCIATES   1:25
                10/22/86

(NORTH S

BACK VIEW OF -

EDGE OF OF
TAIL OPENING

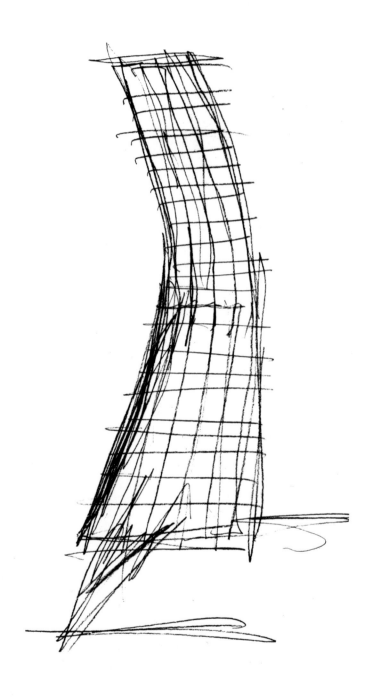

Gehry's architectures attract our attention; they characterise the space in which they live and become the sign of our age, in exactly the same way that has happened with other eternal architectural structures from the past, the pyramids, the Parthenon, the Colosseum, etc., which have reached us with their forms and their language as icons of civilisations now disappeared. But Frank O. Gehry's buildings, with their strong personalities, do not live for rituality, for sacredness, and even less for conformity in human action, but rather they exist to bear witness to the passing of time, to affirm that movement is not a concept extraneous to architecture, that the fun aspect of a project can be present even in buildings whose function today is primarily that of prestige. An example of this is the Nationale Nederlanden office building in Prague (1992–96) which has two tower forms on its main façade, known as Fred and Ginger. In fact, Gehry was inspired for the façade of the building by a well known still from a musical in which Fred Astaire and Ginger Rogers danced as if floating in front of the movie camera. The idea of movement, of the dance, of Ginger's flowing dress, has inspired Gehry for this building, the head office of an insurance company; Gehry has transformed the two dancers into two towers, one, Fred, cylindrical made of reinforced concrete in a single column, the other, transparent made of reinforced concrete and glass with a series of pilotis, Ginger. Halfway up the towers, a balcony overhanging from Ginger stretches out towards Fred: they are the two arms of the dancers, photographed and immortalised in that dancing instant in the Dancing House. All Gehry's work in recent years can be described as a metaphor of movement, of the energy released from daring, light forms, which hover as though weightless.

In the towers in Düsseldorf we again find the lightness of the dancing figures, but if we observe the three buildings from close by, one red, one silver, one white, we note the quality of the materials used, the solidity of the structure and its adaptability to the environment: 'how the sunlight rotating around them and the sound of the wind enveloping them contribute to making the architecture live'. Another magical and captivating work is the sculptures positioned with subtle wisdom beside the Fishdance Restaurant in Kobe in Japan, which make the location particularly charming and attractive. The vitality and dynamism of these volumes are in some ways comparable to the architectures of means of transport, cars, fast trains or aeroplanes. Nevertheless, it is clear that Gehry's metal surfaces under torsion transmit above all a sense of liberty, typical of artistic sculptures, yet they are not influenced by the fascination of industrial culture that was so admired by Modernist architects. Gehry's architectures allude to movement with generous forms, with tense and dynamic lines, alternating with soft and sensual curves, containing exciting spaces. Observing these projects makes us wonder if the future of means of transport, particularly the car, still needs to remain firmly anchored to archaic, rhetorical forms, conditioned above all by aerodynamics. The auto-mobile, auto-immobile will be a means of transport capable of establishing a closer relationship with the surrounding environment; it will be capable of changing skin, of transforming itself along with the changing climatic conditions to guarantee the comfort of the occupants as naturally as possible. Frank O. Gehry possesses a creativity with no cultural or architectural confines. His works are eternal sculptures that transfer the architectural innovation of our age.

ndini

'The urban scene has a precise objective: it consists in the project for the beautiful and the forms of public spaces. We refer to this utopia of the beautiful in the city with the idea of going beyond the Late Functionalist idea of urban furniture. The squares, the streets, the markets, the walkways and their layout designs must be considered as aesthetic works, as fragments of external theatre endowed with emotional and anthropological meaning, able to be profoundly involved with the inhabitants, to be stages for citizens. The architect, the designer, the artist, the set designer, the graphic artist, the designer of lights, these are the operators of these integrated works, whether large or small. So-called modern and contemporary urban furniture arrives from a whole other culture. It really seems that its constitutive elements and objects have been progressively castigated and sucked dry, leaving it the sterile role of arid functions, as arid as the daily life that the man of the megalopolis lives in its flat one-dimensional repetition devoid of rituality. Benches, bins, canopies, buses, kerbstones, flower-boxes, etc. are like cold shipwreck survivors in an urban reality that rejects them and quickly transforms them into waste. To rediscover its profound motivation, the roots of its being, urban design must draw from and connect to pre-industrial cultures. In substance, the furnishing of the city must be set design.'*

¬ L. Parmesani (ed.), Alessandro Mendini. Scritti, *Milan: Skira, 2004, 192*

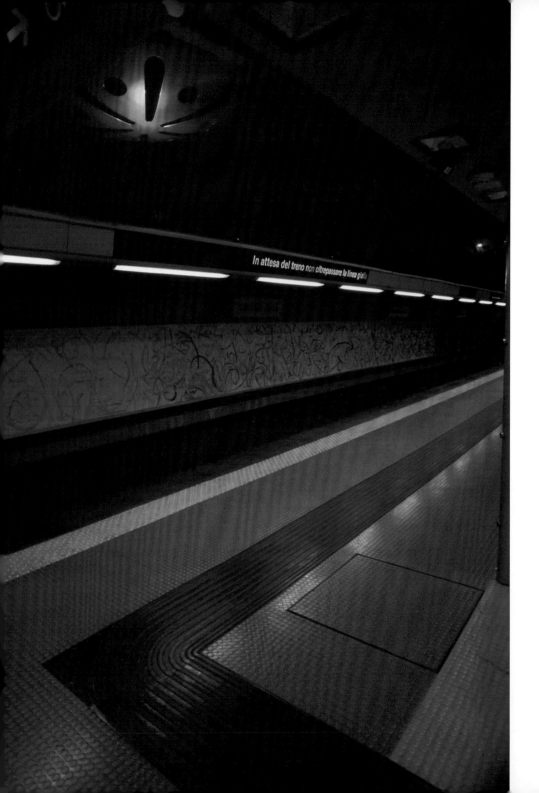

With his project for underground stations in Naples, Alessandro Mendini has adapted perfectly to the spirit of the city. With a careful eye and skilful mastery he has visited and given colour and music back to districts now suffocated by chaos and everyday indifference. As a director he has directed the actors, making them play the role and games of the location. His projects arise from local culture and architectures. Mater Dei and Salvator Rosa stations fit into the city as places of attraction and reflection for the users of the underground, and not only for them: a stage on which the architect/set designer, with the collaboration of artists, opens up a dialogue, also through the other three stations, Quattro Giornate by Domenico Orlacchio, Museo and Dante by Gae Aulenti, with spectators/passers-by invited, as in the rooms of a museum, to a spectacle that does not leave them indifferent to the changes in the Neapolitan urban fabric.

Alessandro Mendini has stepped onstage with an exceptional cast to interpret such a difficult and demanding role masterfully, bringing to it the joy, colours and emotions of a city that for millennia has retained the charm and the role of a capital of creativity. This type of scheme enables the city to embellish itself with places of art in what the specialists call the 'non-locations' of the city.

fuksas

'... urban planning is of no use; rather, I could say that the urban planner as understood in the traditional sense no longer exists, he is of no use any more. We will have to accustom ourselves to envisaging the famous "context" in which we work as by now nothing more than a sum of obstacles and difficulties. We should consider chaos as an integral part of the urban process. Rather, I would say as something of a provocation that chaos is the true order and so-called order can only produce disorder, understanding chaos to be the natural disposition of structures, and contrasting it with the military-type urban model.'

'... my real obsession is landscapes, such as Uluru/Ayers Rock in Australia, the atolls of Polynesia, the enormous dunes that are formed and dissolved in the deserts, icebergs, the islands....
What has always fascinated me is the beauty of the absence of form, the imperfection of beauty. I have always wondered how we can manage to make architecture without form, without there being a dimension, not only geometrical, but complex.
That is why I believe that artists, even the worst, are better than architects, because they always start out with a vision, while architects never talk of this, but always talk about a project.'

¬ *Massimiliano Fuksas*, Frames, Barcelona: Actar editorials, 2001, 128, 283

Fuksas' city allows disorder as a natural form of sublime order, in which the loss of control of institutions and the unbelievable growth in the new means of communication bring about a social fragmentation, transforming every individual into a small enterprise. A molecular enterprise that moves in a setting in continuous ferment in the maelstrom of the megalopolis.

The megalopolis is the modern representation of nomadism: the aggregation that shifts, is continually modified, is something supple.

Fuksas is keen to make a distinction between megalopolis and metropolis, where the former no longer possesses a centre, while the latter is polycentric, and, although it can still be considered the location of modernity, at the same time it is also the historic city, as Manhattan is to New York. The megalopolis, on the other hand, is a form of city that extends over the territory without either limits or confines, in continuous evolution; a tide in which differences and associations merge, though leaving a permanent sense of conflict.

The shifts in the megalopolis take on unpredictable trajectories, like navigation, but the means of transport are still archaic, as Fuksas observes. The car and the aeroplane burn highly polluting fuel and alter the ecological equilibrium irreversibly.

Only the development of technology, for now only observable at its embryonic stage, can change reality and avail itself of the 'net' to organise life in real time.

For the moment this scenario still seems far away and will probably not entirely cancel out the need to move by mechanical means. It is therefore necessary to consider that, while architecture is a fixed presence that adapts itself to a context that changes over relatively long periods of time, cars are volumes in movement that go through very diverse unchanged locations. A car that travels the roads of a tropical city could be radically different from a ski-car amid the snows of Oslo. Or it could be transformable according to the characteristics of the territory. Not only respect for the environment, but also the capacity to adapt to the different conditions, these are the challenges of a new form of mobility.

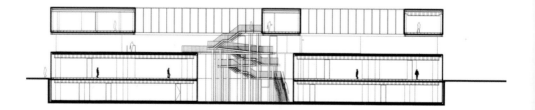

Antonio Citterio

'At the basis of the project for Hotel Bulgari lies the search for the difficult balance between the rigour of the design of the space and the evocation of rich atmospheres, achieved through the use of thick, heavy materials such as black marble from Zimbabwe or bronze.
The building in Via Gabba, built in the early fifties, combined with the beautiful design of the street built up over the past thirty years, has been reinterpreted to bring out its graphic composition. The white marble façade expresses elegance and lightness, in contrast with the solid design of the nearby stone buildings, becoming almost an abstract field, against which the windows stand out with their precious black granite eaves and dyed oak frames, with a part of the 18th-century façade, restored and left exposed.
The control over the design has been applied to every detail.
Hotel Bulgari is an example of total design, in which all the elements have been specially studied and planned: from the door handles to the whole façade, from each single piece of furniture to each desk accessory, from the architecture to the glasses, to the fabrics.
The result is an extraordinarily cohesive design, which gives consistence and precision to the environment. Everything you can see and touch is in fact part of an overall concept that is based on absolute attention to the technical detail and is integrated into the form and substance of the service offered, in a more general attitude to an idea of quality that is absolute, full and uncompromising.'

¬ Antonio Citterio

Living in a design studio of particular beauty and simplicity, such as the one designed by Antonio Citterio in Milan, certainly favours the development of creative work, relations with colleagues and clients, as well as transmitting the approach that the architect prefers for a space dedicated to the project. The studio, a 1,200-square-metre property, is located in a quiet street in the centre of Milan.

The well known architect has designed simple, functional and elegant spaces that are large, open, bright and transparent, spread over a number of floors.

The various working areas interact with simple intersections and appropriate furnishings, designed to facilitate communication between the work groups and the prototype laboratory below. In the upper part of the building, connected by a transparent lift, we enter Antonio Citterio's magnificent 'work room', where covered spaces and accessorised terraces create a splendid environment that can be lived in throughout the year.

The attention to detail and the ease of movement between the various environments have a powerful impact on visitors and convey a sense of the liberty and quality of the services offered. The air breathed is that of a prestigious international studio that could be found in the most sought-after locations in any famous city with a taste for contemporary design.

A private design studio, but also one well suited to a high-level public space, like a splendid 'earth or space' station that receives travellers in transit to offer them hospitality and active comfort.

The technology used in all the environments is refined, perceivable and for immediate use; the specifically designed materials are innovative and create the most highly evolved contemporary habitat.

In his architecture and interior design projects, Antonio Citterio expresses a sense of freedom due to his extraordinary capacity to distribute spaces to suit real and rational uses with an optimum relationship between space and object.

The products used are designed by the architect himself, who, like the great masters of the past, designs the perfect harmony between interior and exterior spaces and devotes particular care to the furnishings, which are designed to guarantee a pleasant living environment and the functionality of the entire project.

This is a particular skill on the part of Antonio Citterio, who manages to design private spaces that are suitable for the public without taking anything away from privacy or from the sense of freedom of movement; they also communicate the image of the client company, as in the case of the Hotel Bulgari in Milan, where the Bulgari charm shines through, along with a sense of contemporary comfort that transmits the sense of well-being.

The versatility, modularity and personalisability of the environments are realised using structures and objects that are sectional, adaptable and transformable to suit both regular and occasional needs.

Transformability and personalisability are necessary prerogatives for static architectures and indispensable for dynamic ones. The forms in movement must adapt to any requirement, environment, atmospheric variable and culture of the location that receives them.

Architecture and mobility, conservation and evolution.

mario

bellini

'If Milan is my city, my ideal city is perhaps a mixture of the hundred beautiful smaller Italian cities that represent that idea of the city that was formed precisely in Italy around ten centuries ago and from there spread all over Europe and the rest of the world.

A city where the houses touch against each other to express the sense of community and to form streets large and small, winding or straight according to a logic that is much richer and more complex than that of the road system, a logic whose traces will remain recorded in that way forever.

A city where the houses, with the monuments, the latter the perennial expression of the city-dwellers' pride, form widenings and squares that, with the roads, the porticos, the fountains and open galleries, are the "location" where public life is expressed and almost performed as the necessary counterpoint to individual and private life.

A city not regulated by the pure functional logic of traffic, transport, crossings, income from land and real estate and economic development.

A city that attempts proudly to save the traces and sense of its own history, that considers its monuments as its untouchable heritage and also aspires to transform itself and remain alive.'

¬ Mario Bellini

For Mario Bellini, designing the new Fair in Milan offered a great opportunity to demonstrate, without any hesitation, that he is among the best prepared and far-sighted of contemporary architects.

In the Portello area he has designed one of the most expressive works of architecture of our time.

Indeed, the building created by him with such great passion and technical mastery is one of the most successful and imposing of contemporary urban projects and has had an influence on the architecture of the entire city of Milan. With his project, Mario Bellini has given a precise indication of how our cities can develop by transforming the disused areas into new dynamic, productive building developments that are closely connected with central and peripheral zones (if we can still speak of periphery, that is, commercial parks, urban parks, technological parks, citadels and protected housing units).

As the Milanese architect has shown, these new developments, suited to places with a high urban concentration, are designed by integrating architecture and mobility, static and dynamic volumes, means and systems of transport, dependent upon the location that receives them, just as the location has suitable architectures to receive them. It is a matter of designing the whole system and its functionality, its road system, the admission, parking and clearing of goods and people, all speaking the same language. Volumes that are fixed and in movement communicate with each other and with the main arteries of transit and access to and exit from the city. The system designed facilitates communication, powering economic and social progress. With this major work, Bellini has defined the difference between the activities of architect and designer, between architecture and objects, between dimensions of the city and industrial product; the skilled design of an object in contrast with the continuous process of technical designing and viewing of a work of architecture.

Around 800 metres long, the Portello complex is one of the most important points of access to the city of Milan along the motorways arriving from the North. An infrastructure that goes from south-east to north-west, before arriving at the city's historic centre; a work of similar importance to the Bastioni, the circle of walls belonging to the tradition of the city of Milan. Between the building's two exhibition levels, Mario Bellini has envisaged a long pergola of flowers and plants that are particularly attractive in an almost theatrical way, two glass towers at the intersections with the two transversal roads and a large drum, imposing and celebratory, giving prominence to the whole industrial work of the Milan Fair Centre. A building intended to express the character of Milan to those entering the city, to give the impact of a contemporary metropolis, the Italian capital of the economy and industry, which is, and aims to be, a model of efficiency for the whole of Europe. Mario Bellini has therefore designed a site of great architectural, economic and social interest, an important connection point for meetings between people and exchanges of goods, a place of communication where efficient mobility guarantees the functionality of the whole economic and industrial system, a kind of obligatory motorway intersection, allowing visitors easy access to the entrance tollgates of Milan Fair.

A great work, a great master who has created it, giving Italian architecture and creativity its justified renown, 'Bellini's Portello' is like a large cruise ship made in Italy, that sails and dominates the sea from the height of the towers, with its drum-ship's bridge seeming to give the sailors a sense of security.

Renzo Piano

'Personally, I find that my desire to explore untrodden paths fits in perfectly with my recognition of the tradition. Perhaps this is a European trait, perhaps it is specifically Italian. It is certainly the inheritance of a Humanist culture.

... when I am asked how the city of the future will be, I reply: "I hope like that of the past".'

¬ Renzo Piano, biography by M. Agnoletto, Archimagazine

'The city is the most magnificent invention of our civilisation.

There are four iconic locations in the city: the university, the offices of a newspaper, the most important library and a major museum. They have a thread linking them, urbanity, and the sense of civitas.

All words, concepts and values are born with and from the city, the most extraordinary invention of civilisation. "Even the most unhappy cities have a happy corner" (this is a phrase that Renzo Piano loves to repeat from Invisible Cities by Italo Calvino, perhaps the writer of whom he is most fond).

It is necessary to extend the corners of happiness, to drive away loneliness, the affective desert; deep down, that is what my work is all about.

The Beaubourg, like Osaka airport, the Genoa Aquarium or the Auditorium in Rome or the Potsdamer Platz, these are attempts to create small cities inside the city, where the most diverse people can meet, defeat loneliness, swap experiences.

Because, even in the virtual age, nothing can replace the magic of the physical meeting place, the agora. In developing countries, monstrous cities are being formed and I tremble at the idea of how they will build them in the area of the tsunami. It is those areas of the world where builders of urbanity are needed, and yet they are forbidden cities for international architects, reduced to being domains of the very worse kinds of speculation.

It is our failure as architects and perhaps also our failure as Westerners.'

¬ Renzo Piano, interview, la Repubblica, 26 January 2004

The Beaubourg in Paris or the Nemo in Amsterdam are reminiscent of great ships moored in the centre of the city; Osaka Airport is a highly evolved place for sorting goods and people on a man-made Oriental island; the old port of Genoa is a meeting place equipped to host passengers in transit between the old and new continents. With his architecture projects, Renzo Piano offers a further and significant demonstration of the existing and necessary connection between *architecture and mobility*, between means and systems of transport.

The work of the great Genoese architect allows an understanding of the concept of *transportation design* in the broadest sense, the relationship between *architecture and mobility* that sees means of transport designed to integrate with the urban territory. His work confirms that tradition is the basis for generating innovation and progress. It was Renzo Piano himself who, in 1983, made the Lingotto in Turin famous: the Italian architect created a magical 'crystal sphere' dominating the famous building of the Fiat Group, almost as though reading, imagining and foreseeing the destiny of the automobile company, who still wanted to emerge and surprise with their futuristic architectures and attempt to relaunch the company.

The work by Renzo Piano, commissioned by Gianni Agnelli, creates an avant-garde atmosphere and a dynamic structure, favouring communication and the connection of the Fiat Group with other industrial groups and

84

with the world of culture in the space of the Pinacoteca Giovanni e Marella Agnelli. The spherical room, meticulously designed, is a particularly fascinating place, a 'control room' that looks out onto the majestic scenery of the Alps, one of the most beautiful mountain chains on the planet, and enables the executives to take decisions with the visual comfort of a unique setting. The dynamism of Renzo Piano's architectures recalls our lives today, where frantic movement, real and virtual, marks the time with merciless systematic rigour, making us live at breakneck speed to reach a destination that is not well identified but is always, incessantly, present. Piano's architectures are the most real representation of a scenario of integration between *architecture and mobility*, a comparison between innovation and tradition.

Renzo Piano's project for Fiat Auto again confirms the great architect's capacity to give life to static and dynamic architectures, organising intelligent, feasible 'modular structures' that are reproducible as standard by industry (as we will see below in the concept car designed for Fiat Auto) and superb 'one-off pieces' for single architectural installations. His is an uncommon talent, as demonstrated in his architectural works created in every part of the world, such as the project for the Zentrum Paul Klee in Bern, a pure work that slides sinuously into the green lawn without breaking the harmony of the location.

Zaha Hadid

A concrete demonstration of the fact that women have achieved emancipation in all professional fields is represented by architect Zaha Hadid; with her professional commitment and her rare talent, she has achieved every goal that until recently had seemed to be the traditional preserve of the 'stronger sex'.

Zaha Hadid's superior intelligence and exceptional charm are legible in all her design works; her constant commitment has placed her at the highest levels of world architecture. The project drafted for the BMW production plant in Leipzig (2005) is a unique, dynamic and astonishing work, as is the Bergisel Ski Jump in Austria (2002), which seems to launch people into space, giving them a propulsive force that enables them to fly without limits of duration or free-fall curves.

Her architecture is as strong as her personality, representing the present but projected forcefully into the future, almost demonstrating the need for the architectures of our world, in the not too distant future, to live in a broader reality, without limits of terrestrial spaces and distances. Zaha Hadid's architectures are 'dynamic sculptures' where form and function merge into a single harmonious work that marks our time.

Lucius Burckhardt

The Cultural Landscape

'History is invisible; it can be made visible by means of the monument.

The 19th century was the great age of monuments. The young nations of that time, the Italy of the Risorgimento, the Swiss Confederation, the German Reich fixed their history, or their version of history, with monuments: Victor Emmanuel I the founder, William Tell the saviour of liberty, etc. The premise for this was a certain unity of interpretation.... Today most of these miracles of marble and bronze stand rather obliquely in the environment of the modern city and the desire of politicians to erect others generally ends in disputes and conflicts. Not even an event as clear-cut as the Holocaust was an exception.

For the purposes of commemoration, as the efficiency of the monument decreases, so the importance of the natural environment increases: that of the cultural and historical landscape, whether urban or rural.

The concept of eternal monuments corresponds to our desire to defend the environment in its current state, our fear of any change in this great collective memory, of the transformation of the cultural landscape.

But all our defence of the current state of the environment, all our attempts to protect sites do not prevent transformations. Every time we return to our favourite places, in Rome, by the sea, in the Alps, something has changed, a building has been demolished, another built, and we observe that the place has become ugly, almost destroyed. Why?

Because we are always seeking the eternal "grandma's village", with the farmer leading the ox and the postman arriving on horseback. Yet the environment changes; and it changes on three levels, which we must consider:

– the real place changes. The origins of the change may be natural or anthropogenic;

– the climate changes, production techniques, means of transport, construction methods are developed; and if nothing changes, there is always decadence, ruin;

– the perception of the environment and its meaning changes.

The history of the Romans can be commemorated in the Roman countryside, or else the more ancient history of the Etruscans, or the Medieval brigands, who transformed the aqueducts into castles, or Dutch painters such as Asselijn, or the German ones of the 19th century, etc. The preparation, the presentation of the environment changes according to the fashion of perception and interpretation. The protection of monuments and sites places the accent on just one period. In the Swiss Alps, the great hotels of the 19th century, Righi-Cima, Furca, etc., have been destroyed over the years—all for the sake of the dignity of the landscape. Those that are left, Hotel Giessbach, for example, are now protected with the same justification. In the Ruhr, after demolishing most of the industrial structures of the iron and coal industries, now the remains are protected, especially the extraction towers that were erected between the wars.

I wanted to talk about the commemoration of history in a visible and concrete form, that is, as cultural landscape. The cultural landscape conveys the idea of history, both heroic and everyday. But we are used to seeing this landscape in a stable, or rather eternal form; yet this is impossible: our idea of "grandma's eternal village" is not a valid one.

I would like to begin the reflection on the unstable historical monument, on the cultural landscape as a process to be designed, to be directed. And on the need to leave to our descendants the freedom to make their own history and their own interpretation.'

¬ reflections on the occasion of the conference
'1515. Battle of the Giants in Marignano', Milan, Palazzo di Brera,
Assembly Room of the Istituto Lombardo, 12 October 1995

Demain on ira au vaisseau brisé
pour chercher quelque architecture

1.2

Outside the Centre

For some years now we have been witnessing a redefinition of the city as a collective phenomenon no longer founded upon architectures or planning schemes, but on social and economic relationships that people or groups wish to establish reciprocally. The evolution of these relationships, sustained by the evolution of technology, by the dynamics of communication, no longer limited in time and space, seems to have launched the age of the global village, which now knows no frontiers.

In many regions the elimination of a clear-cut boundary between centre and periphery, between city and country, generates a diffuse occupation of the territory and the enormous extension of the so-called 'metropolitan' space, which is only differentiated by the degree of density, greater in proximity of the centres and smaller in the suburbs.

The term *metropolitan* is therefore extended to include every location contaminated by the presence of man, recognising a common denominator in the ways of colonising space, relatively independent of their intensity.

Artefacts that indicate the presence of man on the territory, including the forms of continuous monitoring of the earth's surface performed by satellites, theoretically prevent the metropolitan density from being annulled completely.

Many architects and scholars are therefore prompted to interpret the urban structure according to a logic that transcends the traditional distinction between centre and periphery. Rem Koolhaas describes the evolution of the metropolis very lucidly and provocatively when he defines it as 'generic'.

The fact is recognised that even in the countryside people tend to live in an urban way and that the city exercises an influence and an attraction on the territory which leads to urban centres being seen as common spaces, shared by the whole population in a broader dimension.

At the same time, we are witnessing a redefinition of the classic relationship between centre and periphery, which is accompanied, for example, by the phenomenon of depopulation of the most central areas. Such transformations are already under way in some cities in America and Asia, which have a kind of hybrid identity. This identity is very different from that of traditional European cities, in which on one hand the centre tends *de facto* to take on a character of mono-functional specialisation (services, tourism, commerce), on the other the enormous expansion of the suburbs has led to many urban areas merging together.

Consequently there is a widespread use of the territory, which nevertheless retains the presence of various centres, understood as zones of greater density, within a phenomenon of diffuse urbanisation. The depopulation of the cores as areas to live is now accompanied by weak signals of the decentralisation of the services and activities that absorb the largest number of employees.

'Rome has won the challenge with the metropolises. Not only architecture, but also cinema,
tell of the relationship between antiquity and modernity. The first ten minutes of Federico Fellini's
La dolce vita *are striking in this sense.*
Architecture must not feel inhibited when faced with the ancient. It must imitate the other
forms of artistic expression. It has the Church and it has the ancient and it must not engage
in competition.
Rome has already won. The equilibrium that has been regained in the relationship between centre
and periphery is successful. To be eternal, Rome must regain its relationship with the sea.'

¬ *Rem Koolhaas, interview,* la Repubblica, *21 April 2006*

As Ingersoll writes in his book *Sprawltown*, identifying the boundary between centre and periphery is becoming a complex matter. The effort, then, should be devoted to reading the past and making it current through a process of awareness creation that gives the architectural construction a collective identity, in whatever place it is located. To free the historic centre of the city from being the appointed place for collective matters could be the adequate response to a new global vision of 'inhabited territory', as happened in the past for ancient civilisations: permanence and changes produce a more complex and concrete dialectic, but one that is a great deal more socially creative for architecture. The culture of ancient Greece lived for centuries within the Roman, the latter went through the Middle Ages becoming an ineliminable material part of it, and so on. It is no coincidence that Ingersoll's book has *Looking for the City on its Edge* as its tagline.

'The ingredients of sprawl, which include tourism, shopping malls, freeway interchanges,
parking lots, telematic exchanges, single family houses and awkward voids, might seem ugly
in general, but... one can recognise good qualities in [them].'

¬ *Richard Ingersoll,* Sprawltown, Rome: Meltemi editore, 2004

1.3

The Road Network

The road network is very often the main artefact present in the territory and the circulation of vehicles is the only visible sign of the human presence in the landscape.

The road network stretches indiscriminately and nearly uniformly over vast areas of the planet's surface.

Roads make it possible to cross with vehicles vast areas that are geographically very diverse; the mobility system of means of transport therefore has a very high level of flexibility, even if the possibilities of using ordinary vehicles are subject to the necessary presence of adequate roads.

In the light of the major urban transformations described above, we may distinguish two main categories of routes associated with mobility on wheels:

• *Traditional cities*

Characterised by short urban routes frequented by a very large number of people at set times and with rare variations.

• *Extended metropolises*

Extended metropolitan routes, frequented by a relatively low number of people, but with unpredictable timetables and itineraries.

Today's vehicles, so-called 'universal cars', are conceived to handle both situations easily and in most of the inhabited zones the relationship between the demands of mobility and the road system is theoretically satisfactory.

Nevertheless, a series of problems associated with mobility can be highlighted:

– in the most densely inhabited zones, the excessive overcrowding of roads has been transformed into a limitation on people's freedom of movement. In industrialised countries, the traditional markets of the car industry, the problem of traffic, with the consequent pollution and waste of energy resources, has prompted society to develop a critical awareness, which tends to 'criminalise' the automobile.

In many cases the road network is hard to adapt to meet the growth in demand; the solution to traffic problems is identified as being a reduction in the use of the car;

– in addition to the problem of the congestion of the road network, particularly evident in the major cities, the developing countries, such as those of Latin America, Asia, Eastern Europe, potential markets for vehicles, have a problem in relation to the quality of these, which can cause problems for vehicles conceived to meet higher road standards. The expansion of markets to the countries of the Third World reveals a problem associated with the reliability of means of transport, which are not conceived for travelling in the absence of roads.

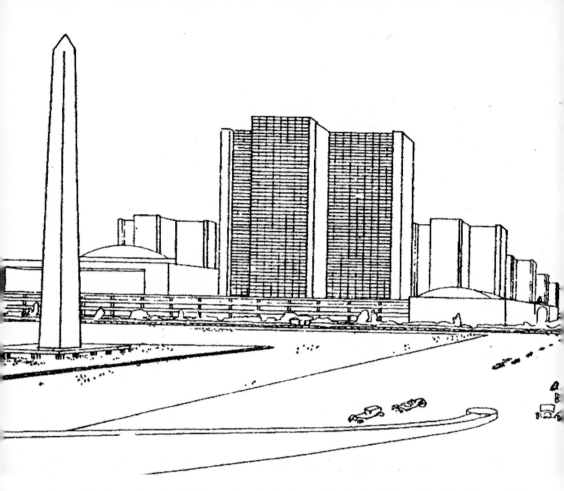

The road is the construction that is most involved in the architecture/mobility relationship. Many mobility problems often derive from the fact that the road is not considered architecture, or at least not an integral part of the overall architectural fabric.

The development of new concepts for the car cannot be separated from the development of total solutions that simultaneously involve vehicle, road and building. Indeed, many cases occur in which the road network is extended up to the heart of architecture.

Airports and stations are complex infrastructures that handle multiple traffic flows and allow exchange between different means of transport.

In these infrastructures the complexity of the project work involved reaches very high levels and allows a relationship between the various means of transport, including the car.

These macro-buildings require planning that is necessarily unprejudiced and open to experimentation, investigation and in-depth programming.

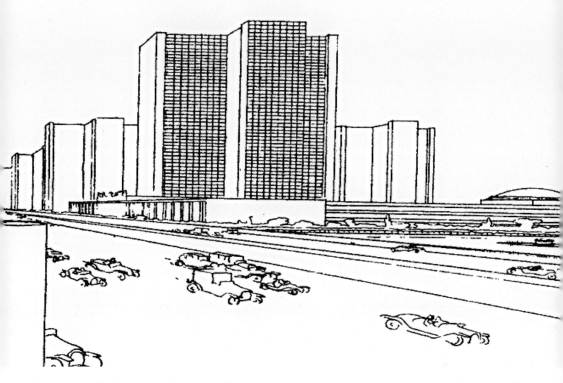

In any event, this discourse could be extended to a certain extent to any construction intended as a place of *permanence* (*architecture*) and of *interchange* (*mobility*).

Research by designers and architects is rarely directed at developing modes of integration that go beyond multi-storey or underground garages—structures, incidentally, that are lacking in most cities. On the other hand, the need is felt to redefine the relationship between *architecture and mobility*, between the road network and architectural constructions, as a closer bond, the reciprocal extension of one in the other. Indeed, few architects so far have handled this theme and in most cases only as a formal provocation. A provocation portrayed very well by U.S. cinema, which in many films (such as the very famous *The Blues Brothers*, 1980) represents the absurd consequences of the intrusion of vehicles into houses, restaurants or shopping centres in a grotesque, liberating sense.

The track on the roof of the Lingotto plant in Turin remains a unique example and, despite the subsequent proliferation of all manner of multi-storey car parks, it is one that still arouses amazement and admiration today.

The Lingotto (Fiat Lingotto Plant, Turin 1914–26) was built at the wishes of Fiat Auto and the Agnelli family to give the company a high profile and to relaunch its car production.

The project was entrusted to Matté Trucco, who designed a testing track on the roof of the building, envisaging a structure of great intelligence, considered one of the first Italian Rationalist buildings.

The main volume consists of a single large block with four internal courtyards.

The difficulty in its construction, combined with the extraordinary decision to use the roof as a location with a functional use, meant that the building aroused great international interest. The Lingotto, in fact, is considered a project that, thanks to the foresight of the designer, anticipated the themes associated with the use of the roof as an active space of buildings, which would only be manifested in the mid-twenties as a major resource for mobility on inflated rubber.

It was a great work that was to become an eternal symbol of engineering and avant-garde architecture, and was even cited by the great maestro Le Corbusier.

In those same years, Le Corbusier drew the curved wall of the ground floor of Ville Savoye (Poissy, France) with a radius equal to the turn diameter of the vehicles of the period, to make it easier for these to enter the garage.

It must certainly be recognised that Le Corbusier had the great merit of realising considerably in advance the need to organise architecture and urban planning projects in relation to the increasing and unpreventable spreading use of the motor car.

The famous *Ville Radieuse* (1929) organises this relationship around pretentious functional bases, that reveal an admiration for the automobile, a fascinating technological object, but at the same time free the urban spaces from the circulation of vehicles, which is resolved with special roads built on pilotis.

Many recent projects construct a dialogue between *architecture and mobility* based on an incisive formal relationship, almost of the advertising type, sometimes ironic.

A very close relationship between the 'automobile product' and the structures to be used for their sale is established in an idea by Alfredo Arribas, in the project that won the competition for the new Smart points-of-sale.

This proposal fits within a perspective of a total communication project, to which the producer and their image, the designer, the history of the genesis of the product, the type of distribution and the advertising all belong.

With this operation there is an attempt to repeat the success of Swatch watches, for a new product, a car 'reduced to the max', which has created a myth, synonymous with a lifestyle, more than a real innovation in mobility.

Alfredo Arribas' idea translates this philosophy for the new and different car product into an architectural form: a gigantic 'set of shelves', as it has been defined, to show the buyer a large number of vehicles.

The showcase for the product becomes an architectural sign.

The customer identifies his own car on the 'shelf', which is also a storage warehouse, and the car is then brought down mechanically to the ground and offered, to great theatrical effect.

Behind the 'shelf' is a large pavilion, a simple arched structure that is reproducible in any location.

It is easy to imagine these structures spread over the territory, in the countryside and in the outskirts of cities: large 'shelves' with cars, marking the location like monuments.

The point-of-sale creates a new signage system, a point of orientation, a communicative network that fits into the urban landscape.

The examples given so far have in common the fact of being buildings *dedicated* to the automobile. The vehicle test track on the factory roof, the period car museum and the car dealer's are spaces that must necessarily measure themselves against their *theme* so as not to be reduced to being banal containers. In other situations, the very form of the building is the consequence of a different way of interpreting the entire programme of production and distribution of the product.

The automobile sector is present in the territory drawing inspiration from symbols of previous civilisation, as in the case of Via Tiburtina in Rome. The Smart tower draws comparisons with the towers of such locations.

1.4

From Car-as-object to Car-as-service

The car is an individual object, synonymous with freedom and autonomy of movement.

The traffic congestion in the most densely populated urban areas has caused a crisis in this way of experiencing the automobile.

At the same time, public and collective means of transport struggle to establish themselves as a competitive alternative to private means, also because they are incapable of satisfying the demands of flexibility and autonomy in movement that are considered by most people to be indispensable.

In contrast, 'micro' cars offer excellent support for this propensity towards individualism.

After many years of resistance to and distrust of this type of vehicle, their diffusion seems to be destined to expand enormously, above all thanks to the Smart project.

Smart meets with considerable public favour because it brings out the individual character of the vehicle; this can hold one passenger at most, in addition to the driver, and does not place current behavioural models in question, but interprets emerging lifestyles. We are therefore inclined to doubt whether 'micro' cars will be able to be considered as offering a long-term answer to traffic problems, which, if anything, they encourage.

Indeed, these problems have now reached such a crisis point as to induce city administrations to introduce new forms of limitation on the circulation of cars. Among the most famous, we can mention the introduction in 2003 of a congestion charge on motorists going into Central London; this can be paid online, by phone or by Pay Point.

Indeed, in many other cities a 'congestion tax' is now in the study phase, the income from which will supposedly finance new infrastructure projects and parking areas.

In India the administration of New Delhi has aimed to develop public transport and, due to the ongoing work to build tunnels all over the city, in 2002 a system of SMS messages was introduced, coordinated by the traffic police, to provide assistance and information on the traffic problems.

It is calculated that 700 million motor vehicles are circulating on the planet, with an increase of 40 million each year and growing. This proliferation is leading to even greater use of environmental resources and it is easy to imagine that in the future too mankind's dependence on mobility will only be partly alleviated by public transport systems or by profound changes in modern lifestyles.

The repercussions on the environment are destined to worsen if the dependence on fossil fuels and traditional engines becomes the cornerstone of the emerging car markets of Asia, Eastern Europe and Latin America. In the coming years radical changes will be urgently required in car production, which will have to win over the traditional resistance to the introduction of new vehicles with low environmental impact, such as zero-emission electric cars for urban use. The very nature of the production core may be influenced positively by the entry onto the market of non-vehicle manufacturers, who will bring in truly new product ideas using *electronic* production infrastructures such as Apple Computers or IBM.

Along with the progress of the automobile product, more in-depth research nevertheless becomes necessary into the relationship of coexistence between the dynamism of the car and the static nature of architecture.

The epochal development of the urban dimension (it is forecast that in 2007 over 50% of the world's population will live in cities) suggests the importance of a greater level of integration between mobility planning and urban planning.

In Europe, in the coming years, this integration could be favourably influenced by the development of the main *corridors* of collective mobility connecting urban and territorial areas.

The extension of high-speed railway lines and the integration between urban, regional and interregional transport networks will lead to the realisation of new interchange nodes capable of being poles of attraction, development and architectural research for the collective urban space.

A greater sensitivity towards the quality of the built-up environment should lead to a critical review of the role of the car, which in just a century has become 'an important possession of almost every family in the industrialised world', according to English designer Ross Lovegrove.

In Lovegrove's view, the ideal car is very different from the Smart car, which must at least be congratulated for having paved the way for a new method of conceiving the architecture of the vehicle, with a better exploitation of the internal space in relation to the overall dimensions; yet this is inadequate in opposing the culture of second and even third cars. The objective, rather, is a single practical solution endowed with a human dimension with no compromises.

Lovegrove's universal car will be capable of holding two adults, two children and their purchases. The expressive objectives of the design will therefore have to take on a new meaning, since the cultural values will be highlighted to adapt to the diversity of personal tastes.

'This will be achieved sensorially and not necessarily physically, by the emotions of smell, touch and electro-biochemical responses pulsating through its hybrid thin film PV synthetic body....

The exterior entering the public domain whilst the interior remaining privately humanistic and atmospheric. As a consequence of such illusion the car could even be programmed to change its colour relative to its immediate environment, therefore responding to the dynamics of Architecture and Nature, in a way which transcends the issues of physicality....

Maximising man, minimising machine. Thus a scenario unfolds where we will see conceptual links between the nature of Architecture, Automotive, Product and Artificial Intelligence evolve into a seamless blend of coexistence.'

¬ *Ross Lovegrove, 'Gaia fotovoltaica', Domus, 800, 1998, 80*

Of course the possibilities of realising such a scenario are associated with the development and application of technologies of materials that are still limited to the field of experimentation.

However, we consider the profound change from a static conception of the object to a dynamic one, from a passive condition of the material to an active one, to be an interesting one.

Transformability is theorised here as an intrinsic aspect of the object, through the nature of the materials of which it is composed and with the aid of electronics.

Conceptually this represents an important step forward with respect to surface transformability, as this is interpreted by Smart, for example, the body of which is composed of interchangeable elements.

The development of advanced materials aims to guarantee a certain degree of transformability through the intrinsic characteristics of the material and not its replacement, which, if anything, will come down to contingent needs.

It is possible that a car of this kind may change the nature of the product into a logic of *service*, or rather of a car *at the service* of the user.

The new car conceived in this way will be able to *recognise* its occupants and self-adjust to meet their needs; but it will also be possible to *reprogram* the vehicle for other people with different habits and needs.

Technology has paved the way for new possibilities, which, though they may still appear remote, invoke a new design mentality, intended to integrate the combined application of electronics and I.T. in the architecture of the vehicle, to improve the quality of service.

The idea of the car *at the service* of individuals could be the first step towards the social aspiration to transform it into a service for the community.

It is utopian to think of resolving the problems of traffic and pollution by reversing the process under way of diffusion of mobility with individual means, which sees the use of public and collective means of transport relegated to critical situations or else regulated by prohibitions on circulation.

We do not believe we are placing the principle of private property in question when we imagine that the logical consequence of the process of transformation of the nature of the car-as-product to car-as-service may lead to new modes of use such as to make individual possession superfluous, at least in some given contexts, associated for example with commuting, commerce or tourism.

This *theoretical model* of a vehicle, transcending the Smart formula in a certain sense, proposes a new style of consumption, custom and behaviour, which is more similar in character to the services of transportation and delivery of goods and information (couriers, motorbike couriers, e-mail).

The 'car-as-service' will be able to be truly competitive and offer an alternative to both public and private mobility, since it will be better connected to the structures of the city (routes, car parks) and capable of performing its mission more cleanly and efficiently.

One possible solution is the concept of car hire (cf. Finizio, G., 'Dal possesso al noleggio' [From possession to hire], *Noleggio*, October 2003). In recent years we have witnessed a phenomenon of transformation from durable and capital goods to service goods. We no longer buy a product for its technical functionality alone, but rather seek a goods item for its validity over time, for its price and for the quality of the service that the manufacturing company is able to guarantee over time.

What increasingly counts is the technological updating, the materials used and the quality of service as a whole. Therefore, a product conceived and designed for a real function by a *design oriented* enterprise that knows how to imagine and produce items for the future, not built only from the standpoint of short-term marketing. Durable or capital goods become real service products and the manufacturing company an enterprise delivering marketing services.

Hire is a modern system that enables a goods item to be used at the moment when it is needed, for the necessary time, only paying for what is consumed. A new freedom and a new culture of use are therefore acquired. The mobility sector, the automotive sector, is important and influences the global economy. The main player is the car, the product of the century, which has brought about a genuine social evolution all over the world. The car sector is characterised by the 'desire to possess', a sort of passionate relationship between man and machine that has to be modernised due to the multiple problems deriving from the improper use of this means. It is necessary to leave the sphere of sentimentality behind and set a more rational course, one that favours a more honest relationship between people, cars and the environment.

It is a matter of planning spaces on the basis of existing architectures, envisaging collection structures for parking vehicles and the distribution of services, and diversified and transformable cars for different and heterogeneous uses, abandoning the craving for possession.

This is to favour a social evolution, also through rental systems that guarantee the constant updating of the product, contributing to safeguarding the environment.

An attractive example of this is Massimiliano Fuksas' project for the New Fair Pole in Milan, where the sense of liberty is expressed masterfully.

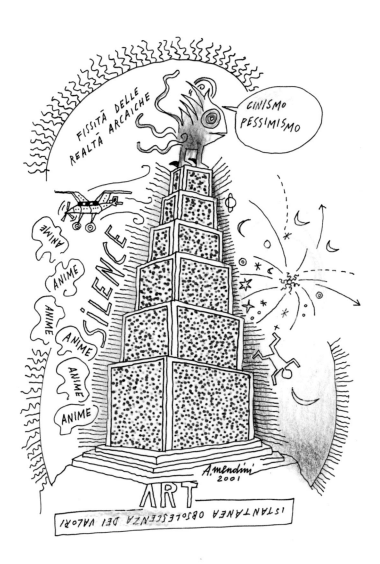

1.5

The Virtual Network

The diffusion of the virtual represents an extension of the space in a dimension that presents a high degree of freedom. The aesthetics of the simulation offer many undeniably fascinating possibilities. Today it is more prudent, however, to speak of the promise that the field of the virtual offers of a fantastic and flexible reality, one that we can experience in our mind, but one that in reality is external to it and can be shared with other participants. The virtual space, which we will still call *city* out of habit, is theorised and feared as a new competitor to reality.

According to some, the consequences of this very recent development will reduce the traditional city to being a mere witness to the past. Its real places will be replaced by virtual places, to allow fast and easy social relations, as well as a vast range of services offered thanks to going on the net. From this perspective, the quality of life in the city will no longer be linked to the quality of its architecture and its building volumes. For others, virtual reality is not in fact a competitor, in the sense that the appearance of this new space does not mean the disappearance of what we possess and know.

In effect, it does appear rather excessive to us to imagine a future in which the demands of mobility and social relations are satisfied without real movement and physical contact. On the contrary, it cannot be ruled out that virtual reality will make what makes it possible and testifies to its origin more precious than ever; that is, the material, which underlies and supports the virtual. Optical fibres are a tangible example of this.

In the previous section we forecast a new role for the automobile as service. This will be possible if the new vehicles can travel at the same time in two parallel and complementary dimensions. The realisation of a virtual network overlapping with the real one will become implicitly indispensable, and the vehicle will be the instrument that will make the overlap legible; it will be the essential medium for the information received. The virtual network therefore takes its place within the form of service that the vehicle renders accessible.

Today various services exist to support circulation on the road network. Information on traffic conditions broadcast via radio is useful to motorists to the extent to which it reaches them quickly and promptly. Its effectiveness is dependent upon the vehicle being fitted with a radio, and the user listening at that moment.

In the future the car will be able to guarantee constant contact with the virtual network, from which it will draw instant information, for instance, extending the control over the road, which up to now has only been observed through the windscreen; this theoretically will give fewer possibilities of error. The car's performance will be improved and connectivity to the network will be no less important than road holding.

Problems of a strategic nature will accompany the traditional mechanical issues.

The designing of I.T. applications must take account of the continuous development of technologies in this sector and identify as soon as possible an expandable system whose updates are easily compatible with the previous steps. This enables us to suppose a relationship between computerisation capacities and vehicles that is anything but obvious.

It will not be sufficient to equip a car interior with the most recent PC, but it will be necessary to identify a new category of instruments, conceived in relation to their purpose, which does not imply their being for single-purpose use and not removable from the vehicle.

Over long years of work, the Philips Design Centre has developed an innovative design method starting from the imperfect knowledge of the emerging needs, or even non-existent knowledge, in the case of needs as yet unexpressed, which are identified and processed through an interaction of research and application models.

To date the automobile sector has restricted itself to embellishing top-of-the-range models with gadgets for data transmission, the direct application of the latest I.T. innovations: DAB radio, Internet connection, sensors and Sat Nav systems, special cards to memorise the user's data and automatically personalise all the settings (seat, climate, stereo). Such innovations represent a full-blown revolution for the automobile, yet they have not yet been extended to the traditional formulation of the architecture of the vehicle.

The task of design will be to identify an innovative conception of the car, which will enable I.T. applications to be transformed from luxury gadgets into a real 'service' for users.

For over a century 3M have been investing significant resources in research, and this has enabled them to have a vast range of innovative materials used by other industrial companies as distinctive elements of their own products. In particular, in the world of architecture and transport (logistics, shipping, road transportation, graphics and lighting, industrial, electronics and communication, security), the vast number and quality of 3M products favour the organic development and functional construction of static and moving forms. Intelligent applications with suitable materials from the US multinational, world leader in enterprise and product innovation, increase road usability and safety on the roads of the urban centres and outside the city. The increasing commitment of the company to design increases the demand from the market. The direct involvement with the 3M Design Center, currently in a phase of considerable expansion, of work groups consisting of in-house technicians, designers and customers reduce costs and time to market, avoiding useless waste of resources. This, *de facto*, forms a perfect strategic and operational alliance between suppliers, designers and buyers, who together foster new product ideas. We have indicated this type of scheme a number of times in the drafting of the text, showing the results achieved by integrated work groups.

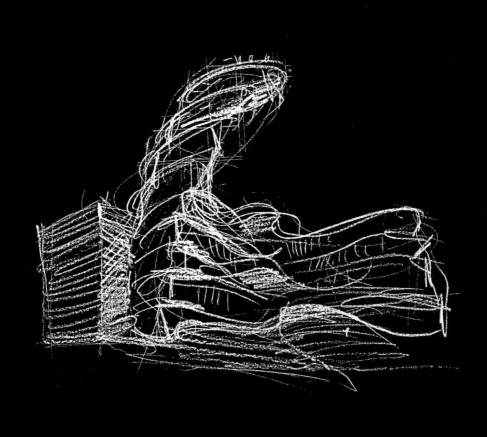

Virtual design has become part of the technical culture of the project, producing high-precision, highly visually effective drawings. These are not sufficient to replace the exciting result expressed by that first design idea, summed up magically in a hand-drawn sketch.

The sketch is the passage from thought to design and gives life to the whole project: it appears and reappears regularly throughout the whole creative process, giving continuity to the development of the work, which takes shape by blending with the material and the technique, while staying faithful to the original idea.

The sketch by Mario Bellini for the Cultural Centre in Turin is the soul of the project, giving life to the work, making it unique and characterising the location that receives it.

The sketch for the BMW Welt building in Munich, designed by Coop Himmelb(l)au, sums up the whole project philosophy and offers further confirmation of a recurrent phenomenon: the contemporary aspect of architecture meets the demand from the car companies to demonstrate business dynamism through the image of their operational centres.

The architecture and functionality of spaces consolidate the brand image, especially of companies with a high technological and design content, such as those in the automotive sector. This phenomenon is an integral part of the history of architecture and the evolution of the company and represents the state of well-being of the most industrialised countries.

A rational relationship between architecture and mobility, between means of transport and city territory, offer a possible solution to—or at least a reduction of—the chaos caused by the vast increase in the number of vehicles.

In this sense, with their architectural structures, car companies offer a valid example of functional integration between static forms and forms in movement.

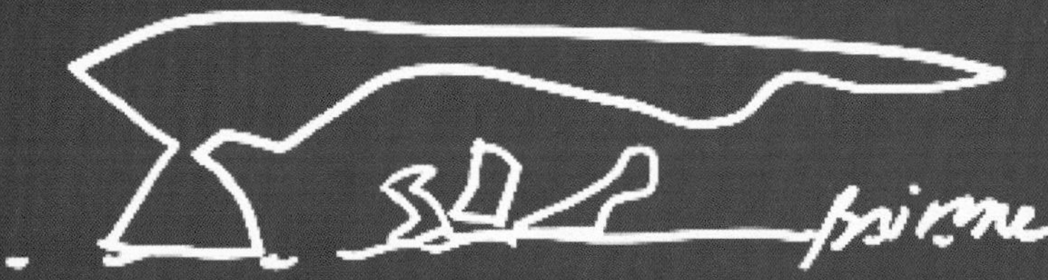

Captions

14   *Mercedes 300 sl* Gull Wing, Museo Quattroruote, Editoriale Domus (photo by endstart)

16   Gino Finizio, *Sketch*

18   Massimiliano Fuksas, New Fair Pole in Milan, Rho-Pero 2002–05 (photo by endstart)

23   Graphic editing by endstart

24   Massimiliano Fuksas, New Fair Pole in Milan, Rho-Pero 2002–05 (photo by endstart)

27   Ole Scheeren and Rem Koolhaas, CCTV and TVCC, Beijing 2008

28   Rem Koolhaas, *Project for a terminal in Zeebrugge* (section), Belgium 1989

29   Rem Koolhaas, *Project for a terminal in Zeebrugge*, Belgium 1989. From top left: level with vehicle access, taxi and bus stop/departure level, public entrance level, hotel and restaurant entrance level, hotel and offices level, casino level, swimming pool and auditorium

30   Rem Koolhaas (photo by Sanne Pepper)

33   Jean Nouvel at the Reggia di Caserta, 2005 (photo by endstart)

35   Jean Nouvel, Agbar Tower, Barcelona 2000–05 (photo by Marc García Rojals)

36   Jean Nouvel, Institut du Monde Arabe (interior), Paris 1982 (photo by endstart)

37   Jean Nouvel, Institut du Monde Arabe (exterior), Paris 1982 (photo by endstart)

38   Jean Nouvel, Institut du Monde Arabe (terrace and interior courtyard), Paris 1982 (photo by endstart)

39   Jean Nouvel and Gino Finizio, Reggia di Caserta, Palatine Chapel, 22 November 2002. (photo by endstart)

40   Michele De Lucchi (photo by endstart)

42   Michele De Lucchi, Triennial Building, installations in the outdoor garden, Milan 2005 (photo by endstart)

43   Michele De Lucchi, Triennial Building, Fiat Café, Triennial, Milan 2005 (photo by endstart)

44   Michele De Lucchi, Project for the Poste Italiane, Piazza Cordusio, Milan 1999–2000 (photo by endstart)

45   Michele De Lucchi, Project for the Poste Italiane, cloister, Milan 1999–2000 (photo by Studio De Lucchi)

46   Frank O. Gehry (photo by Studio Gehry)

48   Frank O. Gehry, Fishdance Restaurant, Kobe, Japan, 1986–87 (photo by Studio Gehry)

49   Frank O. Gehry, Fishdance Restaurant (studies for the construction of the tail of the carp structure), Kobe, Japan, 1986–87

50   Frank O. Gehry, *Design for the Nationale Nederlanden*, Prague 1992–96

51   Frank O. Gehry, Nationale Nederlanden, Prague 1992–96 (photo by Lorenzo Facchini)

53   Frank O. Gehry, Der Neue Zollhof, Düsseldorf 1994–99 (photo by Andy Flenzel)

54   Alessandro Mendini (photo by endstart)

56–57   Alessandro Mendini, Mater Dei underground station, Naples 2000–02 (photo by endstart)

58   Alessandro Mendini, platform of the Salvator Rosa underground station, Naples 2000–02 (photo by endstart)

2 Tradition^Innovation

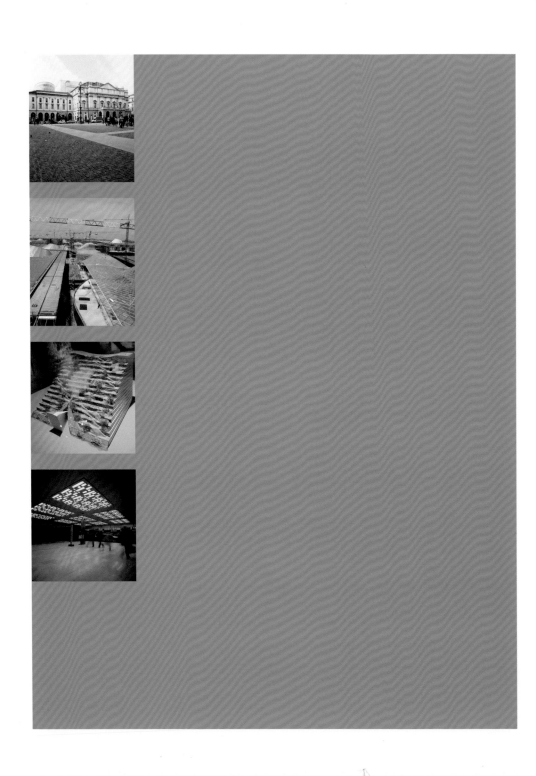

2.1

The Lessons of History / The Temptation of the New

The categories of past and future are at the centre of a centuries-old debate, which sees the concepts of history and modernity set against each other with mutual repugnance. The majority of vehicles in production retain a traditional layout, with rare attempts at overall revision, despite the limitations that are now apparent of a product that has fully entered its mature phase….

2.2

Revising the Meaning of Construction

The car embraces a large number of disciplinary fields at the same time, since it is both an inhabitable space and a mechanical object in movement. For this reason, we consider it interesting to propose a transversal reading of the conceptual aspects and *contaminations* that characterise the contemporary way of designing and constructing buildings, objects ….

2.3

The Size Problem

The *minimal* trend in design, in architecture, in fashion, is not only tension towards the reduction of formal signs to a minimum, but the sign of a profound aspiration to investigate the meaning of things. An aspiration that we do not believe will be resolved in the superficial aspect of products that align themselves with this line, but that we seek *below the skin*, in the profound nature of objects….

2.4

Artificial Light

Light seen as a source of energy never goes out, giving vitality and continuity to the location where *architecture and mobility* meet to establish a dialogue with each other and to create new levels of security that gives comfort throughout the day. The evening, then the night, is handled with renewed functionality, a different and more contemporary atmosphere. To design the locations of light is the prerogative of the chosen few….

2.1

'These individuals, whom we love to define as "teste verdi" ["green heads"], are able to decode and translate these needs into services and products, somewhat in advance of those widespread needs that are transformed into market demands.'

¬ *Gino Finizio, Design & Management course, Milan polytechnic*

The categories of past and future are at the centre of a centuries-old debate, which sees the concepts of history and modernity set against each other with mutual repugnance.

The majority of vehicles in production retain a traditional layout, with rare attempts at overall revision, despite the limitations that are now apparent of a product that has fully entered its mature phase.

• *Tradition*

In cars the revival of tradition is an expanding phenomenon, which satisfies the need for recognisability of an object whose technology is continually evolving.

• *Innovation*

For a long time now progress in the automobile field has been identified with the degree of technological up-grading of the individual components; these lead to a general improvement in performance, but do not alter the general approach to the product, for which the real possibilities of innovation are subject to a revision by all involved of the current architecture of the vehicle.

In designing, the process of innovation may be defined as a response to the incessant appearance of new problems that make apparently consolidated solutions inadequate or outmoded.

Decisions to make changes, whether forced or appropriate, are therefore subject to the definition of precise objectives and take concrete shape in the constant search for innovative solutions to problems old and new.

In the artistic field, and in creative activities generally, innovation is the consequence of the 'innate aptitude of man to incessantly redesign the image of the world', to use an expression by Alessandro Mendini.

This unconditional artistic effort is rarely able to decide the direction of research *a priori*, but sometimes enables surprising results to be achieved.

The creative solution is a kind of escape forward, a product of the sensitivity of artists and designers, but also of entrepreneurs and managers, who are the first to perceive the signals of unexpressed desires or needs.

The creative response is generally developed from the unconscious perception of problems, from a state of mind, from a sense of latent dissatisfaction and not from a purely rational formulation of the terms of the problem. Tradition, on the other hand, is the repetition of solutions considered adequate to given known problems, which have long been understood as being resolved in that way. The dispute between those who claim the need for a continual search for the new at all costs and those who maintain the perennial values of tradition sees the categories of past and future set rigidly against each other. Many fear that tradition naturally resists the most profound innovation, which subverts known schemes and yet represents an unknown, since it is apparently indifferent to tried and tested solutions. Let us not forget that, if on the one hand the design gesture contains the idea of transformation, the establishment of a new order within itself, on the other hand this does not rule out *a priori* that it can also occur through the recovery of memory. The car is a relatively new object and undoubtedly a mature product, for which it is now possible to talk of history and memory. The characteristics that define the automobile can be described through a consolidated model, with respect to which rare and moderate attempts at transgression are recorded.

After all, this complex product does not seem to call for changes to be made to the consolidated model solely for change's sake. The present configuration of the car appears to be perfectly complete. From this perspective, the space for innovation is only justified as a response to clear problems deriving from the use of the car:

traffic out of control in urban centres, pollution above warning levels and increasing safety and security needs. It must nevertheless be underlined that innovation—at least superficial innovation—nevertheless offers an 'irresistible temptation' that is considerably supported by the market. In synthesis, we consider that the challenge between innovation and conservation in the automobile cannot be separated from certain important questions:

– Has the car-as-object truly reached an intrinsic level of perfection such as not to require a revision of its profound nature, in the face of evident general issues threatening it (pollution, resources, traffic)?

– To what extent can technological progress trigger radical conceptual changes in the car? Do the invasion of electronics and the increasing use of IT. represent a revolution or simply a sophisticated improvement?

– Can the creativity of designers force the evolution of the automobile concept towards solutions constructed starting from and in favour of new modes of behaviour? Can the leap forward be, *de facto*, mainly the result of a creative gesture?

The answer to these questions paves the way for the development of new concept vehicles, but this must not preclude the possibility of developing what would be an entirely new conception of the automobile. This theme can be explored experimentally, through projects that this research attempts to support with arguments and observations of a theoretical, methodological and interdisciplinary nature.

Tradition

The theme of memory has had an overbearing presence in industrial design starting from the radical experiences of the seventies. It was initially the expression of a widespread feeling of rejection of industrial modes of production.

In the eighties this attitude evolved into the criticism of the primacy of Functionalist reasoning, which, due to the Modern movement had condemned history without any right of appeal.

The crisis of Functionalism left space for the revival of history as a repertoire of forms to enrich the object with formal and affective values. The most important aspect of this phenomenon, going by the name of *Post-Modern*, lies in the recognition of the importance and independence of form, the added value of the object, not necessarily associated with function. In the nineties the problem was revisited from a different point of view. The diffusion of information technology was accompanied by the widespread use of objects with forms that were not *mechanically* the consequence of their use, but the purpose of which was to improve communication between user and object.

The industry and designers have long sensed the need for recognisability of objects; the development of forms pursues this objective, which ultimately translates into commercial advantage.

Many intellectuals tend to interpret this phenomenon in relation to the social and political events of the last decade, marked by the so-called collapse of ideologies.

The return to tradition and the desire for recognisable forms responds to the psychological need for sure points of reference, for certainties that are not found in the socio-political and religious context.

In the field of the design disciplines, the recovery of memory is an instrument to give a form to *newly invented* objects and services, such as the majority of electronic devices, to respond to the need felt by people to find again the recognisable signs of a collective memory, of an orientation and psychological support in the everyday environment, in the places they frequent. The recovery of the forms of the past is a phenomenon that takes on multiple facets and meanings in the car, including the maintenance of elements strongly associated with the traditional image of the car itself and, in a certain sense, born with it, such as the instruments for driving, first and foremost the steering wheel, the form of which is intuitively associable with its function. Technology has enabled analogue instrumentation to be transcended, yet instruments with dials are still preferred to analogue displays. Then on the formal level there is the whole sporting tradition and all the icons associated with the myth of speed and aerodynamics. All these elements have become part of the tradition of the car and contribute to defining its nature, to the point that they will now be hard to abandon.

The same discourse can be extended *ad absurdum* to also include the element that most characterises the car, its indispensable element, the wheels, which must be four.

On this subject, it seems to us to be interesting to note that in science fiction cinema, cars, which no longer require wheels, are represented with bodies that make their descent from today's cars recognisable.

Consider, for example, Luke Skywalker's car in the very first *Star Wars*, or the menacing vehicles in *Blade Runner*, up to the more recent taxi driven by Bruce Willis in *The Fifth Element*.

The recovery of memory, besides being understood as the maintenance of the most characterising elements, can also take on the character of a genuine citation, also of objects not directly associated with the world of the automobile.

The boot, the folding top, natural materials such as wood and leather, belong to the sphere of objects that give the car a character of almost domestic elegance, of physical and psychological comfort.

The return to expressly *retro* forms perhaps inaugurates the first *historicist revival* in the world of the automobile.

It is no coincidence that this phenomenon is occurring precisely at a time when the technology under the car bonnet is less and less comprehensible to users. The memory of historical forms and lines, but also the recovery of old philosophies (*Multipla*), reassure the user and make the car recognisable. Memory thus becomes a patrimony to be interpreted, to the point of being—as the scholar François Burkhardt affirms—an instrument, a method for those working on the project.

This is possible if the tradition is redefined in present-day terms and not as a rejection of the contemporary, but as a factor of development. History is thus transformed from being a heavy form of conditioning into a laboratory for experimentation. This is demonstrated by the research, experimentation and designs of architect Eduard Böhtlingk (cf. Kronenburg, R., *Portable Architecture*) and by many other young designers involved in the field.

'The transformative potential is associated with the potential of the artefact, which through simple gestures and movements, allows itself to be used differently'.

¬ *Giorgetto Giugiaro,* Panda *Fiat Auto designer, 1980*

Transformability responds to a number of functional criteria, as in the case of the interior of the *Panda*: the car was supposed to display personality traits in order to repeat the success achieved with other utility cars such as the *Topolino, 500* and *600*.

The design requirement was: 'we need a car in jeans' and, following an idea from Giugiaro on the interior, it was declared: 'For the solution for the rear seat, I started from the deckchair. When I proposed keeping the cloth under tension using transversal tubes, I confess that I did so with a certain anxiety ... the same solution of the tube was transferred to the dashboard and the pouch, which proved essential, very capacious and very light (besides the tube, a simple sheet of covering applied to the plate).' (from Bosoni, G., Confalonieri, F.G., *Paesaggio del design italiano 1972–88*, Milan: Edizioni Comunità, 1988).

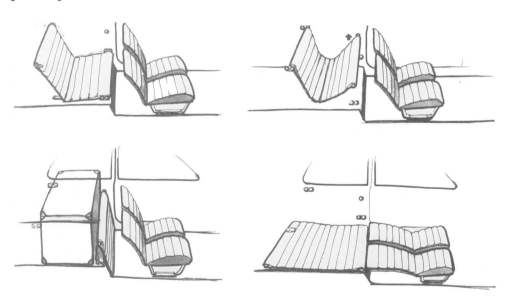

Passing time ages the architecture of cars, and they become obsolete, awkward old ladies to be inserted on the noble list of period cars.

The *Panda* is simple, transformable and adaptable; it is the car we seek when we want to design one suited to our times. The *Panda* is the authentic model of the utility car created by the designer of the last century, Giorgetto Giugiaro, who has been capable of reading the industry, the market and of producing innovation.

Innovation

The car has often been compared metaphorically to an organism composed of a skeleton (structure), a muscle system (mechanical organs) and a skin (body). For a long time the car's progress can therefore be identified with the progress of these individual components, which lead to a general improvement in performance, but do not alter the overall approach to the product.

It follows that the space for innovation has been considerably reduced and the car can feel fully entitled to be considered a mature product.

For this reason, it seems to us to be interesting to shift the observation onto the *relationship* between the single components: skeleton, muscles and skin.

It is undoubtedly a complex, evolved relationship; one that is hard to jeopardise, but one that nevertheless shows some weak points in the aspects associated with comfort in a broad sense, that is, everything that concerns well-being and the physical safety and psychological security of the occupants.

The prevailing architecture of vehicles is the result of a now consolidated configuration that includes various components, linked by a solid relationship of a *mechanical* nature.

This configuration can only be reconsidered and questioned through a different approach to research.

The recent writings of Andrea Branzi investigate the potential changes that arise from a new way of relating to science, aware of the indeterminate approach that characterises contemporary thought.

Designer and design theorist Branzi claims that this indeterminate approach has produced a form of 'atheism' in relation to science, from which there arises a 'downy' form of thought (the so-called 'fuzzy logic') that represents our reality well.

According to Branzi, the rejection of the bases of science and the agnosticism of its theorems are the sole possible philosophical condition from which to derive models of ethical behaviour; these models are no longer related to Good or Evil, but more similar to soft processes of self-regulation with respect to environmental conditions.

These processes, typical of many electrical appliances, are the clear expression of a technological culture based on the capacity to relate to the context through a sensitive and active interface.

In this work we have already made reference to the hypothesis that in the future the characteristics of materials will be capable of mediating our relationship with objects and between these and the external world.

Materials are a territory of research, investigating the roots of the perceptive experience, to construct a more profound, lasting dialogue with things.

This dialogue is built starting from the designing of material qualities, colours and textures, in anticipation of rather than following to the definition of the performance features of the object and the fixed and moving architectures. The project for the colour and its possible transformability over time, with suitable materials, characterises locations and at the same time makes them flexible and adaptable to meet new demands, as

well as making them easier to maintain; this seems to be a problem to be taken very seriously, in view of increasing labour costs.

Not only plastic, but also malleable woods, thermoplastics, natural fibres transformed into biological plastics, fall within the scenario of 'designed materials'.

This hypothesis seems to cancel out the relationship between the current components of the vehicle and could reshape its boundaries, making them extremely unstable and hard to recognise within known categories.

The suspension of the search for new languages, for constantly upgraded forms, is a prelude to the activation of different operating conditions, which proceed through the dismantling and reassembly of the car's present repertoire of formal and functional solutions.

The criteria that guide this operation aim to increase the relational capacities of the product, which becomes *generic*, open to the contaminations of traditionally separate functional spheres.

In the paragraphs that follow the reading is proposed of objects and architectures that pave the way for an innovative conception of the shell that surrounds them.

These architectural choices, as for the Cour Visconti in the Louvre, which will not be covered but remain visible, are the architectural choice forcefully asserted by architects Mario Bellini and Rudy Ricciotti, in search of a 'soft, non-violent integration' between a resolutely contemporary architectural project and a historical site.

The new museum spaces at the Louvre will be covered by an 'iridescent cloud' that, emitting a discreet diffused illumination, will gently float above the museographic presentation. Thanks to this 'luminescent cover', there will be the perception of the façades of the courtyard from inside the new museum spaces. From inside the rooms, visitors will be able to admire the interplay of folds and waves of the roof, which will give the whole scene a poetic charm.

In this—as in other examples—the *shell* is the instrument that establishes new potential relations, even if sometimes only symbolically.

The characteristics of the *shell* make it similar to a membrane and suggest the path towards a relationship of self-regulation with the exterior that in some ways, like an egg, synthetically sums up the features normally provided by many components.

From these observations it may seem that the path towards innovation coincides with an increase in complexity. In reality, the design effort should lead to discerning more boldly how to make the car simpler and more essential, capable of performing its own mission without waste.

2.2

'To proceed by "contaminations" is a characteristic that is widespread in various fields of human action today. To contaminate means to go outside of the closed and protected perimeters of uncontaminated things, to make them react together in order to obtain unexpected and more complete results.'

'The architectural object, the object-painting, the object-sculpture and the design object are paritetic forms, whose alternate world fortune is associated with the capacity of the respective formative processes to take up the existential tension of mass society; the more the latter is sensitive to the disciplines, the more they, hybrid and contaminated, succeed in translating into explorations of life.'

¬ *L. Parmesani (ed.),* Alessandro Mendini. Scritti, *Milan: Skira, 2004, 705, 707*

To what extent is the car object or environment? Perhaps the car is an object that contains an environment. The definition of the disciplinary field is important. The car embraces a large number of disciplines, to varying degrees. The complex nature of this product makes it at one and the same time an inhabitable space, a micro-architecture and a mechanical object in movement, which must meet precise and rigid performance requirements. On this subject we consider it interesting to propose a transversal reading of the most innovative aspects that mark the contemporary way of designing and constructing buildings, objects and cars. An analogy can be found in the new way of conceiving the 'meaning of the construction', which we find in various disciplinary fields, whose relationships have undergone profound mutations. The fall of the 'synthesis of the arts' has in a certain sense paved the way for a new form of dialogue between the various disciplinary and design spheres: contamination, a spontaneous phenomenon now generally taken to be a design tool.

Alessandro Mendini emphasises how the phenomenon of contamination has been transformed into the only way to regenerate the arts, particularly design and architecture. This does not mean—the author specifies—that temporary transfers have to be made, that the painter will start to design houses, the fashion stylist to paint, the architect to do a little of everything. Rather, there is a methodological translation, which sees design as a form of art and art as a form of design, conceptually different from the traditional synthesis of the arts. The artistic aspect of design work—according to Mendini—therefore resides in the capacity to frame the project in an aesthetic relationship with the other disciplines through interwoven methods, in order to obtain original results.

From this perspective, the designer/artist is called upon to make a new cultural commitment, to represent the world, as traditionally proposed by the Classical artistic disciplines and today taken up as a form of project.

For the designer (and for the 'green heads' described in paragraph 2.1), the sensitivity in drawing inspiration and stimuli from the external world becomes even more important than the capacity to forecast, with respect to which the project has lost faith and manifested clear limitations. In the field of architecture, the role of the individual as 'sensor of the future' was focused upon and examined in depth on the occasion of the Biennial of Architecture in Venice, entitled 'The architect as seismograph', recognising the designer's role as going beyond that of pure specialist. The scientific conquests of recent decades have led to a renewed attention towards natural morphologies and their representation. The discovery of fractals, for instance, has revealed the existence of a flexible and unpredictable order, on the verge of chaos, in the natural world.

In architecture and design this new vision has led to the revival of the theme of the forms of nature, as a phenomenon going beyond fashion and trends, but it has become a strategy of behaviour that has developed a different 'meaning of construction'.

Architect Paolo Portoghesi describes this phenomenon as a new form of organicism; this has not been consolidated into a trend, but is free to expand in the most appropriate directions to recreate in the objects constructed a natural scenario and the specific requirements of self-regulation of living organisms.

Buildings and things become increasingly similar to *cells*, whose membranes regulate the osmotic relationship with the exterior.

The analogy is not only conceptual, but also formal, and is manifested in the search for nervated or smooth details, for joints created in assonance with natural forms. In architecture this way of building is extremely clear in the works of personalities as diverse as Renzo Piano, Santiago Calatrava and others.

Now we will attempt to read the developments and effects of this inclination to reconfigure the products in the sectors of architecture and design, particularly to understand what repercussions they may have upon the car.

To conclude, we wish to stress that the observation of the material scenario of the construction is particularly important if we think that the car belongs to it—as we explained at the beginning—as architecture or inhabitable space, and as a design object, since it is capable of movement in space.

The Inhabitable Cell

'I go in search of depth, of meaning, of poetry, of pleasure.
This means making architecture today. Not stretching the city into places where it is not. It means
starting from a reality and then enriching it.'

¬ Jean Nouvel, interview, Domus, 800, 1998, 17

The international specialist press presents a panorama increasingly crowded with tapered and ovoid forms, made possible by the application of advanced technologies. In these architectures the simple exhibition of technical virtuosities, typical of a high-tech language, is transcended by the search for more profound symbolic meanings, the possible expression of a renewed language of design; as in Böhtlingk's project for the inhabitable cell, the *'Markies' Special Caravan* (1986), in which it is possible to live in an uninhibited way and personalise the environment to meet one's own needs, work and leisure time requirements, or the relationship of living in harmony with nature. The expressive values of architecture seem to take priority over the cold exhibition of technology, the result of a mentality that tends to make the value of the architectural work coincide with the degree of technical upgrading. The architectures in which formal aspects are the immediate consequence of the application of the best available technologies, or in which expressive solutions using aesthetic-formal or conceptual values are not experimented with, immediately appear old-fashioned when the market offers new products that are often not very innovative in their contents but updated in their appearance.

Architectures in the form of enigmatic geometrical solids, such as the sphere and the oval, metaphors of unusual sources of inspiration such as the egg or the whale, represent a concise gesture filled with symbolic meanings. They are immediately legible and convey an idea of uncompromising integrity, as in the project realised by the Mecanoo group for the ING Head Offices in Budapest in 1994. An organic mass, apparently suspended on the glass roof of an old building, over the traditional geometry of which it is superimposed, ignoring it, defying the laws of gravity. The construction of a membrane closed onto itself, with a uniform surface, which almost attempts to detach itself from the ground to protect its precious, fragile human content, releases a strong emotional charge and at the same time is revealed as the natural product of an attitude of defence in relation to a context that is sometimes truly hostile. This is a very clear characteristic of the car, which must truly guarantee an adequate degree of protection and safety to occupants under a vast, unpredictable range of conditions. In this sense, the architecture seems to manifest at a conceptual and formal level something that must happen in the car by necessity. In the twenties, Le Corbusier had compared the house to a *machine à habiter*, a machine for living, recognising a criterion of functionality and the elements for a new architecture in industrial products, ships, aeroplanes and automobiles. Today we observe an evolution of design criteria in every sector towards a new organicism that generates inhabitable cells; paradoxically, these may be fixed or in movement, architectures or means of locomotion. In architecture the obvious technical impossibility of representing volumes that hover in the air and that conceal their structure is resolved, in poetic-compositional terms, by intersecting these forms with volumes or parts of buildings that also completely envelop them and *protect* them, without ever completely hiding them from sight, so as not to give up the powerful attraction they inevitably generate. A significant example is the Jean-Marie Tjibau Cultural Center in Nouméa, in New Caledonia. In the project by Jourda-Perraudin and Foster for an auditorium in Toulouse, the large ovoid volume of the congress room, covered in stainless steel sheets, seems to float in the void contained in a metal cage that contains it and protects it without totally hiding its shining presence, almost as through representing a modern technological *nest*. For the Bibliothèque Nationale in Paris in 1989, Koolhaas imagined a parallelepiped in which the public spaces are defined by the interstitial void that is generated between the five suspended volumes housing the spaces of the library proper, which have been defined as 'floating embryos in the technological placenta'. The recourse to ovoid volumes is far removed from the research in the field of decomposition and fragmentation, typical of Deconstructivism, even if it probably shares with this research the theoretical matrix that is developed starting from observation of the complexity of reality, comprehensible only through theories that come to grips with the concept of chaos. Nevertheless, we believe the designer who has recourse to such a demanding formal and structural choice does not intend to express this complexity through the fragmentation of the architectural shell, which creates effects of disorientation.

These architectures manifest a strong sense of 'concentration' of the mass through a totally 'entire and pure' volume, not even lightly scratched by the functional demands of the interior, sometimes deformed in their length (*blob*), and possibly suspended from the ground, which almost disturbs it with its banal flatness, but at the same time is indispensable in order to underline the independence of these *organisms*.

The form of the egg catalyses the attention. The space it generates subtends the existence of a centre, a core. The building takes on the character of an object in space, free from constraints.

This sense of freedom makes it similar to the car, with respect to which it foregoes the possibility of movement, but expresses a sense of suspension from the external physical context.

The tower created by Sir Norman Foster, one of the most authoritative architects of the century, for the Swiss Reinsurance Company, is a sculpture—popularly known as the 'Gherkin'—that characterises our frantic 'torpedo' age. In the film *Basic Instinct 2*, the protagonist is not the famous U.S. actress Sharon Stone, but rather the Gherkin, as everything revolves around it.

London, which hosts the Gherkin tower, is the theatre for a new way of consuming cinema; architecture is an integral part of the set design and the colours merge with the material, form and architecture of the interiors to support a film that does not have a *raison d'être* unless it is founded upon this scenography of the city. London seems to be a place reconstructed for new contemporary cinema, where the director finds real sets, already prepared, meaning the most efficient service for finishing on time and at the envisaged cost. The recent film *Match Point* by Woody Allen, intelligent and passionate, launches a modern approach to the 'whodunit' genre, which itself originated in the mysterious fogs of the London of another age.

norman foster

The Ovoid Object

The ovoid form is common in many sectors and is more easily associated with objects than with buildings, such as industrial silos, for example, the shape of which meets exclusively functional requirements.

And it is precisely in objects that we encounter it increasingly frequently; from inflatable objects, to lamps, to all those objects endowed with an enveloping body that acts as protection and as an interface with the exterior.

Nevertheless, there is a distinction between the aware use of the ovoid form and its appearance as a product of manufacturing processes.

Almost all glass lamps are reminiscent of a bud, but only Castiglioni's *Brera* lamp is distinguished by its obvious intention to represent the egg, which symbolically contains light.

In many recent projects, the forms seem to allude to a *soft* relationship with the user, a friendly relationship, tactile as well as visual, very different from functionalism, which belongs to the communicative logic of traditional appliances, for example.

Computer-aided design and manufacture excessively amplify the morphological transformation of products and, in synergy with electronics, simplify the modes of access and use of these goods, having abandoned the myth of functionality expressible mechanically through the form of the object.

The *Oz* refrigerator and the *Zoe* washing-machine, conceived by the Zanussi Industrial Design Center, are the result of research that takes the product back onto a more natural plane. A refrigerator that opens like a shell, a small, round washing-machine with zoomorphic feet testify to a stage of the process of transformation of the product, which, thanks to *fuzzy* electronics, is suited to individual needs and revives formal archetypes inspired by nature. The *Eye* camera by Ross Lovegrove has a compact, closed, oblong and rounded form, made of an elastometric material that makes it soft to the touch. The object acquires meaning in the physical relationship with the user's hand; it offers itself to tactile exploration and is pleasant to caress and hug, according to the idea of sensuality as a medium for the aesthetic experience.

The organic aspect of forms does not follow a formal intent, therefore, but rather the interpretation of gestures through which the user establishes a relationship with the object, as well as using them, as happens in Ron Arad's famous circular bookcase, which can be moved like a wheel. The formal and structural simplicity of objects conceived in this way is also the response from designers to the increasing need for comprehensibility caused by complex technologies that users do not understand.

iMac, the well known personal computer by Apple, came about in order to speak a simple, direct, immediately perceivable language, aimed at demystifying the technological object that participates in an idea of global communication, through an almost manic attention to every detail: from the design of the interior, which is visible through the ovoid transparent plastic body, to the colour of the surfaces, to the texture of the rigid structural elements.

The synthesis between structure, form and communicative immediacy is not only suited to highly technological objects. It finds an exemplary application in many furnishings, even rather dated ones, which now belong to the history of design. From the futuristic models of Joe Colombo to the historical pieces by Pesce and Bellini for B&B, to the enigmatic *Egg* armchair produced by Bonacina. This piece, designed in 1957 by Nanna and Jorgen Ditzel, consists of a wicker shell and is midway between a furniture item and a micro-environment contained in an essential form. The uniqueness of this object is underlined by its pendant structure, which differentiates it from any pedestal-type seat. It is of course an image that has no direct relationship with the car, but communicates very effectively the protective and double character of this object-environment, which we can find again in a very legible form in the *Citroën 2CV*, produced in 1936, where the sense of protection expressed by the ovoid shape in the centre of the car alludes to the protection that humans receive in the mother's womb.

The simplicity of the car, supposedly inspired by Le Corbusier, makes it a founder model of modernity, the symbol of modernity that provides autonomy of movement for the owner and the people and objects they wish to transport. The rural dimension of this car, which was used in that period by families in the French countryside, contributed to the economic and social evolution of the whole territory. Fiat Auto, manufacturers of some of the most recognised utility cars the world over, such as the *Panda*, *Uno* and *Punto*, have never succeeded in finding an alternative that could usurp the supremacy of this simple family car produced by Citroën.

We need only recall a quote by Gianni Agnelli: 'I have no regrets about the life I have led and the objectives I have reached; I am only vexed that it was not me who had the 2CV produced'.

In architecture too the ovoid form regularly returns to give harmony to the project or functionality to its roofs, which are used masterfully as theatres of art to transfer culture.

To sum up the ovoid object, we refer the reader to the *Brera* lamp designed for Flos by Achille Castiglioni.

The Bubble Car

In car design, the bubble car is the result of research in the field of aerodynamics and safety. The bubble car is capable of absorbing impact, with a mechanical shell that protects passengers and guarantees greater interior space considering its limited dimensions. The increasing diffusion of MPVs encourages this design tendency, which develops starting from technical and performance requirements, which the forms of the body have come to emphasise and which, with perhaps rather excessive tones, have led to talk of a revolution in car design. The proximity of the shape of the car to that of a sphere does not subtend the ideal proximity to the most precise and perfect form in nature: the sphere. Rather, it follows from the combined efforts and the compromise between the demands of aerodynamics and ergonomics.

Unlike the visionary projects by the French Rationalists of the late 18th century (Ledoux and Boullé), the widespread contemporary ovoid, even if precise, does admit deformations, nervations and porosity on the surface, which make it more similar to the cell, the living organism. Today the reference to nature is more instinctive, less filtered by reason, compared to the Enlightenment tradition.

The diffusion of ovoid forms in the car can be read above all in the light of the interior space they generate. A space that is undoubtedly protective, unique, privileged in comparison with the outside world, in which one may feel like an embryo. At the same time it is a space where the surfaces enveloping it avoid being perceived as a whole, yet are well present. In this space it is not possible to free oneself from the presence of certain enveloping confines.

It is comfortable and claustrophobic, protective and absolute.

In nature the enclosed space is the space of the cave, the ancient shelter. In this meaning the sense of protection, almost sepulchral, is prevalent over the ideal perfection of the geometrical form. But the car is more similar to the cradle, the first cabin, the immediate replacement for the mother's womb, where we experience our first sensations, where we eat, play and sleep without interruption for long months.

The car is an environment to live in, also equipped for kinetic uses, as the cradle often is.

In its ideal configuration the ovoid volume is a space whose shell cancels out any distinction between walls, ceiling and floor, becoming a single enveloping surface. It is difficult to imagine a fully realised space of this kind.

The unidirectional force of gravity makes a plan of reference necessary to make it usable. Destined to remain an ideal space, it is configured in constructions as necessarily imperfect. Its form is nevertheless so evocative of the beauty of a natural object that, even if partial and incomplete, it evokes its quality.

'In all projects that employ the cellular form, the aspiration to create something new is perceivable, or rather to realise an architectural organism that preserves a form of life, the embryo of a subsequent development, the metaphor of the new dawning architecture. The oval membrane becomes ideally invisible to reveal the birth of a new era for architecture and design.'

¬ *Alessandro Villa*, Appunti di viaggio, *1995*

2.3

The Size Problem
Luigi Formicola

'To take possession of space is the first act of every living thing, men and animals, plants and clouds, an elementary manifestation of equilibrium and continuity. The occupation of space is the first test of existence.'

¬ *Le Corbusier,* New World of Space, *1948*

This is what Le Corbusier wrote, expressing a clear vision of the designed work, understood as an incessant desire to take possession of space; a desire that, starting from the primary arts, architecture, urban planning, sculpture and painting, succeeded in achieving its pre-established purpose through the stimulus of constant creativity. Le Corbusier's studies on the *Domino* system from 1915 and his theorisation of the *Modulor* in 1948 had already brought the problem of the mass-produced industrial dwelling into the spotlight in the first half of the 20th century. The perfecting of new techniques and new materials in the early 20th century, such as reinforced concrete, enabled Le Corbusier—but also many other designers—to realise what they had theorised: *l'unité d'habitation* in Marseilles (1947), synthesising a new and revolutionary idea for a living space, also sought to offer a response to one of the many questions raised by the Modern movement on the urban planning issue. A new vision of space is promoted, one that is dynamic, inhabitable and standardised, minimal, where minimal does not indicate solely and necessarily small, but above all functional, modular, repeatable and therefore rational. *Simulate, codify, materialise, dynamise* become the watchwords of a new system in which users find themselves absorbed in the discovery of a new space that no longer needs any definition. *Domino* is based on a construction with a reinforced concrete skeleton on six cubes that raise the construction from the ground. The distance of the floors, and therefore the total height of the building, is determined by the structures of the industrially produced doors and windows. The walls and partitions consist of light fillings. As for the industrial object, in the same way the mass-produced house, through a rational construction system, must reduce costs and realisation times, yet still meet the requirements of inhabitability and usability of the space: the attempt to optimise the process of production of architectural construction according to the industrial model theorised by Ford in the automobile field. Le Corbusier's insights and the tendencies begun by him shifted the attention of the architects of subsequent generations towards increasingly experimental and extreme directions, availing themselves of the innovations achieved by industry in the sector of plastic materials. It is in this framework, therefore, that we may insert the 'Visiona 1' event, promoted by Bayer in 1969; on the occasion of the Cologne furniture fair, the event had called upon designers of the calibre of Verner Panton, Joe Colombo

and Olivier Mourgue to promote the potential of a new material in the domestic sphere, plastic, but also to publicise a new domestic lifestyle.

'Today the problem is posed of offering furnishings that are substantially autonomous, that is, independent from the architectural shells, and co-ordinable and programmable so as to be able to adapt them to all today's and future spatial demands.'

¬ *Joe Colombo*

Joe Colombo's thought clarifies the point of departure of his whole formal and functional research into the furnishing project, which shifts from the project to the product and from the product to single units, in an attempt to meet those industrial demands that are defined, but above all the needs of a market that is continually changing.

The evolution of the modern world, however, does not move in step with the forecasts and theorisations, however futuristic these may be. *Habitat Futuribile* [Futuristic Habitat], for 'Visiona 1', designed by Joe Colombo in 1969, is an experimental project, a prototype of futuristic habitat inspired by the concept of a new way of living with a constantly evolving reality. Thus there emerges the proposal to forego dividing walls. The usable space is managed using movable units, genuine 'machines for living in', equipped and freely distributed so as to be adapted quickly to suit every demand. The units, *Central Living, Night Cell, Kitchen Box*, are not conceived as furniture items/objects, but as full-blown coordinated machines: a dynamic system to experience a completely free space.

photo by Rodolfo Facchini

Between 1971 and 1972, from the experience that he had accrued with previous projects in the field of 'furniture' components, Joe Colombo created the *Total Furnishing Unit*. Displayed at the exhibition 'Italy—The new Domestic Landscape' held in 1972 at the MoMA in New York, it was composed of four units, *Kitchen, Cupboard, Bed and Privacy, Bathroom*; these structures, which are autonomous and differentiated, have a flexible dialogue with typologically different environments. When combined, they occupy a surface area of just 28 square metres.

It is interesting to note that the *Cupboard* unit is also used as a division between two environments and the *Bed and Privacy* unit accommodates all the functions of home living: sleeping, eating, receiving guests or retiring into a specially designed private space.

The interior layout design project is conceived as independent units capable of being positioned inside the inhabitable space according to a modern, futuristic conception: a furniture machine designed to meet the demands of a new, less conventional type of user, keen to interact with multifunctional and hyper-technological objects.

The research and experimentation conducted by architects in the sixties and seventies into the designing of interiors was also considerably encouraged by industry and by the introduction of new technologies and new applications of traditional and innovative materials onto the market.

In those years the contaminations from distinct sectors, such as transport, also defined the lines of tendency within architectural and interior design.

The dream of the conquest of space, after Neil Armstrong was shown on the moon's surface, in a famous photo in 1969 that was seen all over the world, and the consequent illusion of an alternative life on other planets, also supported by a vast number of movies, also undoubtedly influenced Kisho Kurokawa.

The project for a capsule for a single tenant, which must have inspired certain settings in Luc Besson's 1997 film *The Fifth Element*, is just one example of the research conducted in the late sixties with the aim of reducing inhabited space.

Inside the cell each element is conceived and made to comply with the most rigid rules of functionality, almost simulating the habitat of a vehicle or, even more futuristically, of a space vehicle.

The capsule designed by Kurokawa is built using fireproof resin, and occupies 3.3 square metres, compared with the 15 square metres of a normal hotel room. These capsules are stacked on a steel frame, forming the hotel. Distributed over two storeys, access is gained to their interiors through front hatchways. Through a redesigned and rationalised architecture, people can succeed in living the experience of alienation from an increasingly complex and dynamic reality in which the inhabitable space, transforming it into a luxury item, is the prerogative of the few.

However, as the 20th century drew to a close, mankind did not manage to *take off* for new worlds and the problems of home living and architecture kept alive the debate among designers, who endeavoured to give a concrete response that took account of the questions associated with urban infrastructures, transport systems and above all respect for the environment. The phenomenon of complexity therefore became the central theme of designers' reflections at the end of the eighties: among these, Rem Koolhaas defined this system as 'culture of congestion'.

In 1995 Koolhaas published S, M, L, XL, in which the quantitative, but also qualitative approach to the problems faced is evident: the urban space, the domestic space and architecture in general return to being a problem of scale.

The inhabited space generates forms and emotions, attractions and illusions.

The house in Rotterdam, built in 1988 by Rem Koolhaas, sums up this concept very well. The outside and inside spaces follow each other in an interplay of reflections and transparencies, cancelling out the distinction between one and the other. The patio, like the rest of the house, succeeds in defining a space with interior simplicity and essentiality in which the minimal consists of absence, reduction, the conscious choice to remove. The idea of movement, of a rhythm marked by the visual suggestion of a minimalist space that opens towards the outside, establishing a new dialogue with the environment, is at the basis of Koolhaas' design methodology, which in this building—as in all his other projects—operates according to the rules of 'dematerialisation' that he himself theorised. A new opportunity therefore appears on the horizon: to destroy the confines—and not only the physical ones—of architecture. It could be the new response of contemporary architecture that, supported by new technologies, is finally freed of all the construction constraints that Vitruvius had summarised in the term firmitas, liberation that prompts us to imagine, and therefore to realise, architectural constructions in which new experiences can be lived that are akin to dreaming; the attainment of a new dimension that expands the perceivable space, creating a subtle interplay of illusions between real space and imaginary space; living the space without any limitation, transcending the interior/exterior, visible/invisible barrier and redesigning a system of architectural infrastructures within which moving from one place to another is less and less indispensable, modifying the architecture/mobility relationship, to the point of turning it upside-down.

In 2000 Massimiliano Fuksas designed the Third Millennium House.

As suggested by the title, the theme imposed upon the Roman architect the use of a language that was not only spectacular, but futuristic. Every custom in the designing of the domestic space is transcended and the user is ready to live the space in tune with the environment, yet without necessarily devaluing the technological contents that progress imposes upon us.

The views of architectural work are virtual realisations.

Like many other contemporary designers, Fuksas chooses the instrument of virtual reality not only as a means of control and instant modification of the design idea, but above all as communication and direct experience of the visitors/users who find themselves inside an imaginary space, but one very similar to a coming reality. This new system of design and visual perception opens up new scenarios in the field of architectural design, which accelerates its process of development using media tools and languages.

178

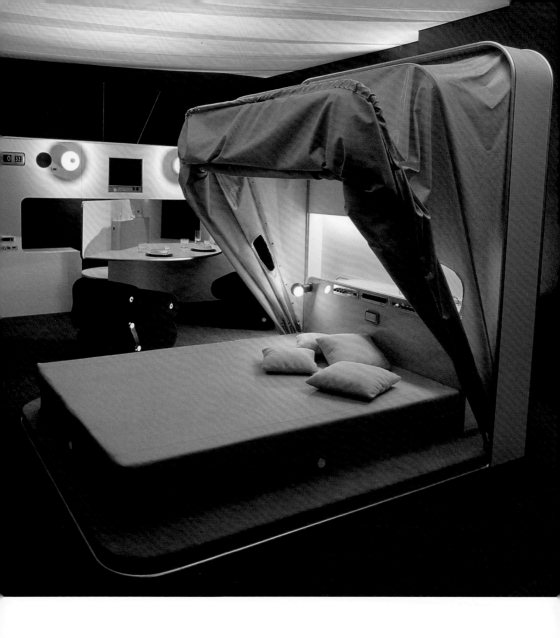

Architecture breaks through all frontiers and transcends its own limits to become a movable experience in time and space. Experience thus becomes one of the key words of contemporary design work.

Whether we are referring to cultural activities hosted in spaces designed for the public at large by great designers or we are talking more simply of small-scale commercial activities, the watchword is 'experience', whether performative, sensory or interactive, provided it is experience.

Car design is not immune from this *diktat*. The current tendency, shared by the most important car companies, is to seek distinctive elements in various sectors, from fashion to entertainment, from advertising to cinema, from architecture to interior design, that can make the car product not only more competitive, but above all more in tune with the habits and needs of contemporary life. In this scenario, the link between *architecture and mobility* has been consolidated and the relative contaminations are increasingly frequent. It is permissible, therefore, to ask whether designers busy in the resolution of this complex problem take due account of the most critical aspects of the mobility project, first and foremost the whole size question, thus succeeding in realising what Le Corbusier hoped for back in the early twenties.

'If the problem of the home, the apartment, were studied like a car chassis is studied, our homes would quickly be seen transformed and improved. If houses were built industrially, mass-produced, like the car chassis, unexpected, but healthy, definable forms would quickly be seen to rise up and aesthetics would be formulated with surprising precision.'

¬ *Le Corbusier*, Vers une Architecture, *ed. by P. Cerri and P. Nicolin, Milan: Longanesi & C., 1973, III,* Occhi che non vedono… le automobili.

On the following page, Massimiliano Fuksas' project for the Milan-Rho Fair confirms the foresight of the French master years later.

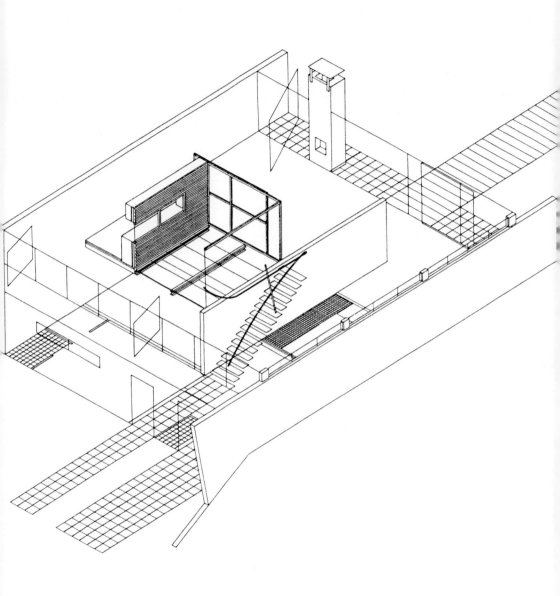

2.4

Pietro Palladino

'Artificial light contends with the urban scene; it creates its own architectural syntax and its structural potential constructs the city at night.

In this context of reference, an intense nocturnal mobility is articulated, since social and community life have moved into the evening hours.

Fixed and moving lights define the night-time image that enlivens the public space of contemporary cities.

It is on the territorial level that today collective interests and identities are formed. It is on the territorial level that the desire to live well is manifested and most social consensus is rooted. Quality of life, traditions, culture and history meet on the territorial level. To illuminate our cities well means enhancing the territory, increasing the quality of our lives.'

¬ Pietro Palladino

Artificial Light

As we have said, the car is being transformed not only in its form, but also from a durable consumer item to a capital and service item, to be used by individuals and enterprises.

The use of the car for private use, in the urban centres with a high concentration of population, must always be kept under strict control. The inclination is to shift the concept of the 'car as possession' to that of the 'car as service' for public and heterogeneous use.

This phenomenon, which is already in the process of transformation in the urban centres, does not influence the relationship that vehicles, private and public, must have with other systems and means of transport, infrastructures and nodes that connect the city with the suburbs or with other urban centres.

Mobility must be planned and continually upgraded; architecture, means and systems of transport, places of concentration and traffic nodes must be integrated and must communicate with each other better.

This consolidates the trajectory of the architectural evolution, increasingly characterised by functionality expressed through new public spaces that go towards a greater 'humanisation' of the location. The city is transformed into the metropolis and changes with the population, who change from a 'local people' to a 'multiracial people' with different needs in terms of movement and economic resources.

In the new planning philosophy, the railway station is a meeting place, a lung for the city, a plaza to stop and spend some time in the comfort of adequate structures, to then start moving again.

An inviting location, an oasis in the city, where a multitude of people are in transit; forms in movement merging into a single, harmonious moving mosaic, made of colours, sounds and light.

Light seen as a source of energy 'never goes out', giving vitality and continuity to the location where *architecture and mobility* meet to create a dialogue and new security that gives comfort throughout the day. The evening, then the night, is handled with renewed functionality, a different and more contemporary atmosphere. To design the locations of light is the prerogative of the chosen few, the true 'masters of light'.

Pietro Palladino is one of these rare designers, technicians and creatives, who give vitality to locations with light, creating a genuine rebirth of the place or the work of art, making them live from their own light. Buildings and sculptures, static and moving bodies are delicately enveloped in light. The rare skill of the designer highlights the peculiar characteristics of the work of art or route with 'illuminating energy', functional paths in environments destined for public services. To go around at night, in the company of the light that caresses the monuments, saved from the incessant traffic, is an activity that regenerates people and gives them new vital energy to face the confusion of the day after. The trail of light, soft and continuous, designed by the colours and reflections of an automobile, like the embroidery of the trembling light of the city, seen from the height of an aeroplane, represents our time; the true works of art of our age, which cannot help but make us appreciate light, though knowing the negative aspects and advantages of progress, technological and social, produced by the forms in movement that enable the people of the earth to be in constant communication.

188

Tadao Ando

Tadao Ando's wise and intelligent Oriental gaze seems to invite us to observe without useless words. Surrounded by a group of disciples, in respectful silence, he observes his latest work, illuminated by his genius. An intense and subtle light crosses Palazzo Grassi, illuminating the temple of art, formerly of the Italian nobility and now owned by a French businessman. The works on display for the extraordinary opening event emerge undisturbed and reveal their splendour caressed by the light of the great Japanese master.

Tadao Ando spreads his wisdom with surprising applications, designing with simplicity and minimal waste of materials. Light, diffuse order, spatiality, access and movement are the most obvious results of his work expressed in temples, churches, museums and places of art, which seem to suggest the necessary order to

be spread and set against the chaos that reigns in our cities.

Tadao Ando could design the road system of a city creating an equilibrium between static and dynamic bodies that from light, as a source of energy, draw the information necessary to make it function in a hypothetical ideal mobility.

From among the many splendid architectures designed by him, we will restrict ourselves to showing that of the Sayamaike 'Museum of Water' in Osaka, where the space is animated by natural energy: the sound of water and the light reflected in it transmit a feeling of well-being and full harmony between people and nature.

Captions

130 *Sant'Antonio da Padua*, Museo di Capodimonte, Naples (photo by endstart)

134 Mario Botta, Restructuring of the Teatro alla Scala, Milan 2002–04 (photo by endstart)

136 Hanselm Kiefer, Installation, Archaeological Museum of Naples, Naples 2004 (photo by endstart)

138 Nigel Coates (photo by endstart)

139 Nigel Coates, National Centre for Popular Music (detail), Sheffield, UK, 1996–2001 (photo by Studio Coates)

140–141 Nigel Coates, Project for the National Centre for Popular Music (panoramic view of the phases of construction), Sheffield, UK, 1996–2001 (photo by Studio Coates)

143 *Rome eternal city*, Piazza del Campidoglio: one of the two Dioscuri Castor and Pollux, placed there in 1584 *(photo by John Blanchard)*

144 Giorgetto Giugiaro, *Drawings for Fiat Panda*, Fiat Auto, 1980–94

145 Giorgetto Giugiaro (photo by endstart)

147 Nomad matting by 3M (photo by Marcello Sebis)

148 Rear-reflecting films for road safety, 3M Scotchprints (photo by 3M)

150 Massimiliano Fuksas, New Fair Pole in Milan, Rho-Pero, 2002–05 (photo by endstart)

152 Massimilano Fuksas, Ferrari Research Centre, Maranello 2001–03 (photo by endstart)

155 Eduard Böhtlingk, Markies Special Caravan, 1986 (photo by Studio Eduard Böhtlingk)

157 Renzo Piano, Cultural Centre, Noumea, New Caledonia, 1993–98 (photo by Studio Renzo Piano)

158 Norman Foster (photo by Norman Foster & Partners)

159 Norman Foster, Swiss Reinsurance Headquarters, London 1997–2004 (photo by John Blanchard)

160 Jean Nouvel, Agbar Tower, Barcelona 2000–05 (photo by Marc García Rojals)

162 Nanna and Jorgen Ditzel, *EEG* suspended armchair, Bonacina, 1957 (photo by endstart)

164 Piero Della Francesca, *Montefeltro Altarpiece* (detail), 1742, Milan, Pinacoteca di Brera

165 Achille Castiglioni, Brera, 1992, Flos – Jean-Baptiste Mondino institutional campaign

167 Graphic editing by endstart

168 Emilio Ambasz, *Project for Fukuoka Prefectural Hall* (model), Japan, 1990–2004 (photo by endstart)

171 Le Corbusier, *Project for Maison Domino*, 1914–15

172–173 Fred Scott, *Technology, Naturality & Civilisation*, 1998

174–175 Joe Colombo sitting on the *Elda* armchair, 1963 (photo by Rodolfo Facchini)

176 Joe Colombo, *Rotoliving*, 1969 (photo by endstart)

179 Joe Colombo, *Rotoliving and Cabriolet-Bed*, 1969 (photo by endstart)

3

Transportation Design, Design

3.1

Lines of Evolution of Vehicle Architecture

The project for a new vehicle architecture cannot be separated from the knowledge of lines of trends and certain innovative projects that have represented the fundamental stages in the process of innovation that has been underway for some years.

It is not our intention to go back over the history of the automobile, nor to offer a complete overview of the *concept cars* and *concept ideas* that are produced every year....

3.2

Concept ideas

Riccardo Dalisi – City   Michele De Lucchi – Small

Isao Hosoe – Personalisation   Toshiyuki Kita – Easy

Mario Bellini – Inhabitability   Alessandro Mendini – Colour

Richard Sapper – Elegance   Jean Nouvel – Distances

Antonio Citterio – Sportiveness

3.3

From Car Design to Transportation Design

Ermanno Cressoni

Innovative Thought

Design for Innovation in Enterprise

Design around the Idea

Architectures in Movement: Travelling Cities

Static Architectures and Dynamic Architectures

Photography

Mandra

3.1

Lines of Evolution of Vehicle Architecture

The project for a new vehicle architecture cannot be separated from the knowledge of lines of tendency and certain innovative projects that have represented the fundamental stages in the process of innovation that has been underway for some years.

It is not our intention to go back over the history of the automobile, nor to offer a complete overview of the *concept cars* and *concept ideas* that are produced every year and presented at furniture shows or in the specialist press.

Nevertheless, we do think it useful to dwell on certain projects that focus the attention on a new spatial conception of the car interior.

In general, the greater attention devoted to the comfort and spaciousness of interiors is coming from a new segment of vehicles, the so-called 'MPVs', large, medium and small. The trail-blazer for a new generation of vehicles of this type is the Renault *Espace*, presented in 1984.

If the prototype Alfa Romeo by Castagna in 1913, the Fiat *600 Multipla* from 1956 and the famous Volkswagen van are excluded, in the past car companies have not devoted much attention to the theme of a vehicle with the spaciousness of a van, but with the dimensions, performance and style of a saloon.

The first models to explore this concept were successfully commercialised in the USA by Japanese companies, such as Mitsubishi (*Chariot*, 1975), Toyota (*Tercel*, 1982), Nissan (*Prairie*, 1982) and Honda (*Shuttle*, 1985), although it was only following the success of the Renault *Espace* that all the companies devoted their energies to manufacturing this type of vehicle.

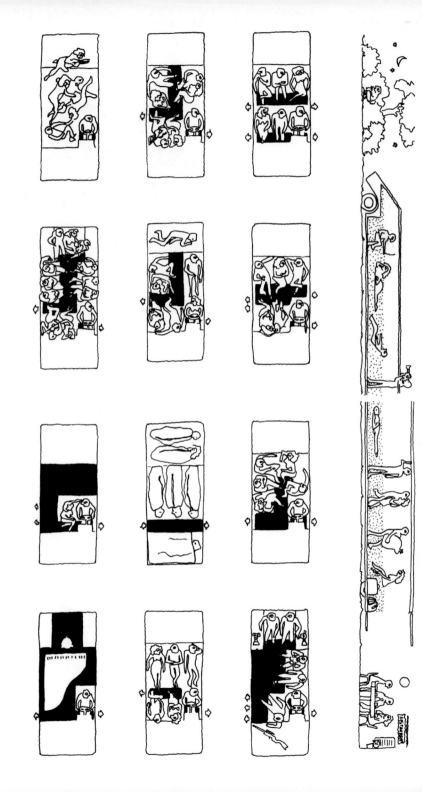

At a distance of some years, we think the *Espace* was both an excellent example of a new type of car and a clear expression of a tendency still under way (to increase the height of vehicles in order to obtain a more spacious interior).

This line was also taken on board by utility cars, starting with the Fiat *Uno*, designed by Giorgetto Giugiaro in 1983.

This very successful model fits within a broader area of research to improve the inhabitability of the car, begun by Giugiaro himself with the well known Fiat *Panda*.

Mario Bellini had considered the theme of the inhabitability of the car, presenting the *Kar-a-sutra* project at the 'Italy: the New Domestic Landscape' exhibition that was held at the MoMA in New York in 1972.

On that occasion he presented a car concept totally free from pre-established schemes, challenging the direction of those years to favour the parameters associated with power, speed and opulence to the detriment of interior inhabitability. It is for this reason that today *Kar-a-sutra* is considered the conceptual model of the MPV, even if it did not lead to the construction of any prototype or mass-produced car.

Kar-a-sutra came about as a result of Bellini's capacity to rework the theme of the vehicle in a spatial, architectural vein, free from the customs and constraints represented by the established types.

The body clearly derives from the study of the interior space, where Bellini favours the use of large glass surfaces to put travellers in contact with the external environment. The reference for this project in the automobile field can be identified as U.S. station wagons, of which it represents the natural evolution, with a greater development in height. However, with respect to these, it introduces a series of solutions that were later only to be applied to a mass-produced model with the launch of the Renault *Espace*, analogies concerning proportional and stylistic aspects (by inclining the windscreen the radiator grill is slimmed down and is highlighted by the upright of the fixed front window; a central upright marks the limit of the front part with respect to the large glass rear parts; the rear hatch is almost vertical and the exceptional interior inhabitability is achieved with a completely flat platform that offers extensive possibilities for changing seat positions).

Bellini's solutions anticipated the demands of the market by many years, but above all they accommodated motorists' desire to experience the car as we live at home, as is visible in the Renault *Espace*, the *Megane Scenic*, the Fiat *Multipla*, the *Twingo* and in the *Ecobasic* research project by Fiat Auto Advanced Design.

205

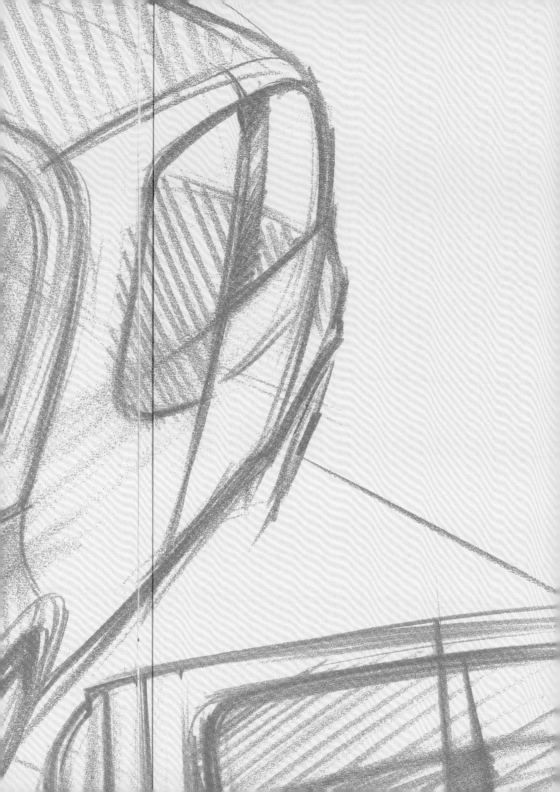

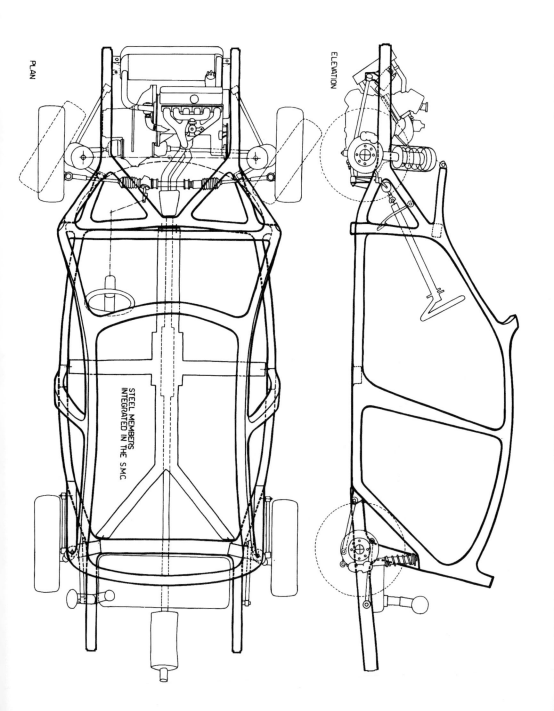

PLAN

ELEVATION

STEEL MEMBERS
INTEGRATED IN THE
S.M.C.

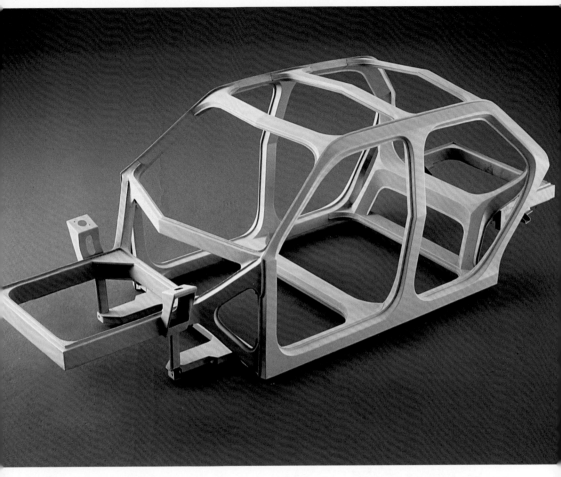

Between 1978 and 1980 Renzo Piano developed a *concept design* for an experimental car based on the separation of the external shell, which was interchangeable in relation to the supporting structure and resistant to impact.

The project, named *VVS*, developed in collaboration with the I.D.E.A Institute in Turin, enabled a car to be obtained that was 20% lighter than traditional cars.

This solution envisages the supporting function being moved further back, into the body of the *chassis*. The structure enables a *frame* to be achieved that is resistant to torsion and can absorb energy during impact, while the body can be lighter, more interchangeable and flexible.

The project, with the architectural part of the vehicle by Renzo Piano, concerns the evolution of the structure that has led to a formal and conceptual model that is still innovative today in international terms, where there is an increasing demand for flexible and interchangeable structures on technologically advanced platforms.

3.2

Concept Ideas

The work of research on the *architecture-mobility* relationship is the prelude to the development of a series of design proposals developed by an interdisciplinary team of designers and researchers coordinated by Gino Finizio Design Management, on behalf of the Fiat Research Centre.

The formation of the interdisciplinary group had as its purpose the extension of the field of study to include the world of architecture as a source of inspiration for a new concept of the vehicle and mobility in relation to the evolution of the contemporary city.

Historically, the city came about as a place of communication and exchange.

Cities generally arose in places near to the natural communication routes—a river, a natural path, an established route—and increased their power on the basis of their potential for exchange—of goods, information, discoveries, and people—with other cities and with the countryside.

The path of evolution of the city is therefore associated on one hand with the increase in exchange, on the other with greater efficiency in communication.

The wealth of Western society is associated with the possibility to communicate, move and interact through different territories.

The mobility of cars plays a key role in this evolution. The value of the car is not only associated with the object in itself, but with the network of transformations that it has provoked: from the construction of motorway infrastructures to the improvement in the operational flows of the production system, to the geo-economic transformations that have, *de facto*, established the primacy of the city as an economic entity producing value and driving progress.

Among the tools at the disposal of the Western collectivity, the car therefore becomes the element that improves exchange and the possibility of communication between people and peoples; this at least until a given moment in the development of our society.

Today we realise that, due to the lack of adequate infrastructures and the car's distribution in excess of the city's physical capacity to accommodate it, this fabulous instrument of individual liberty has reached a critical threshold of functionality.

The increase in the time we spend travelling by car, road congestion, the excess of urbanisation and the absence of a system of control and management of schedules and times in the city have become a dramatically evident problem for the quality of civil life.

From this realisation, it is now possible to offer two sets of considerations.

Mobility is a form of material communication between entities far apart from each other. Alongside it are forms of communication that do not envisage the transportation of goods and people, but only the transfer of energy.

This energy takes on different forms and different values and has significance when it becomes a vocal impulse on the telephone network, a digital image on the computer, sound, voice and whatever else via satellite.

214

The increase in this type of communication is particularly evident and places the community living within the physical confines of the city side-by-side with a second—virtual—community that extends beyond it. Exchanges now take place not only inside a physical location, but beyond the confines of spatial proximity.

The car is the most widespread condensation of technology to be developed by our society. Its objective, to release people and allow communication, is becoming invalidated today by its excessive success. Yet being the concentration of evolved technologies could enable the object to travel not only through physical territories, but also along virtual communication paths. The car would become an agent of communication; if mobile through physical spaces, if immovable through virtual spaces.

The second set of considerations consists of those in which the car is viewed as a domestic prosthesis.

Of all means of transport, the car is undoubtedly the most inhabited. Inside it domesticity is not reproduced in an imitative sense, but as a representation of parts of the home, particularly the living room. This paradox leads us to consider the car as a genuine home, as a cocoon in which the intimacy that is enjoyed is different from the traditional domestic kind, because 'the automobile in its double everydayness does more than stand in opposition to the home: it also IS a home, but an exceptional one; it is a closed sphere of intimacy, yet released from the usual limits of intimacy, capable of an intense formal liberty, a dizzy functionality… an extraordinary compromise is realised: to be at home, ever further away from home. The automobile therefore becomes the centre of a new subjectivity, of which a circumference does not exist, while the subjectivity of the domestic world is circumscribed' (Jean Baudrillard, *The System of Objects*, 1968).

To these considerations, today we may add that the concentration of technology to which we have referred enables the car to become a full-blown technological prosthesis of the traditional house. If it becomes this, then it is likely that it can become an intelligent appendix of the natural workplace and slowly integrate within architecture, taking on its characteristics and compositional categories, taking on forms less associated with mobility, more with the idea of the inhabited journey, both staying in one place through the network and in movement.

These instruments also pave the way for a new use of the car-as-service, for use by a wider public; for example, the public of those people who have an access card to the entertainment and information services offered by the automobile and share the use of this vehicle with others, like members of a club or a more open community.

Riccardo Dalisi – City

The project for the *Slipper* car was developed in 1998-1999 by the students of the School of Specialisation in Industrial Design in Naples on the occasion of the Fiat Auto European Competition for Young People, with the supervision of Professor Riccardo Dalisi. Among the various work groups, the proposal by students M. Silvestro, V. Fontana and F. Molitierno achieved distinction and received the prestigious second prize in the competition.

The methodology adopted and forcefully encouraged by Prof. Dalisi was characterised by creativity. Creativity understood as an incentive to make up for the uneasiness of an imbalance and where the design gesture comes about as a creative response to the dishomogeneousness of a given sector.

Calm, serenity, comfort and familiarity are the feelings that have inspired the project, for a car conceived not only as a means of moving around, but as a space to be able to live all the time, even immobile, as an object that is integrated into the natural and urbanised landscape; in Naples both these elements are very strong. The very name of the project, *Ciabatta* [Slipper], contains the spirit, the sentiment, of a project for a vehicle that communicates likeability and tenderness.

The research work was launched with the realisation of over 200 sketches and cardboard models. From a selection of the most significant ideas, they arrived at the realisation of the actual scale model on the chassis of a Fiat *127*, reclaiming parts of old cars from workshops and building new ones by folding and beating plates mounted on profiles of iron tubing. Two years of work finally led to the realisation of the functioning prototype.

Ciabatta is a polite car, as its creators define it, a car that when it rains welcomes the rain with its umbrella (an electronically controlled rain canopy) and immediately offers its instruments, which are few, essential and identifiable without looking, to the driver.

Its considerable height allows you to enter the car without having to bend down. Access is facilitated by the large door positioned centrally. The seats can be arranged in various ways inside the car, with the possibility of being extracted.

A slow car that can be transformed: the double front bonnet, when turned over, becomes a kind of two-seater deckchair and the rear hatch, when open, becomes a small veranda.

The intention was to create a friendly, pleasant and simple car, perhaps one that was also a little spartan and irreverent. The important thing was to communicate this feeling, this inviting aspect, this playfulness in its transformations and this character in its form.

The result is a car with a smooth line and without aggressive elements, tracing a soft gesture similar to a caress. The interior of the *Slipper* offers passengers a completely different experience compared with traditional cars, a new concept for an interior space. First of all, the clear-cut separation between front and back seats is abolished and the height of the roof is raised well over the passengers' heads.

When the vehicle is standing still, the interior acts as a small study, with a pull-out table under the dashboard that avoids using the steering-wheel as an unintentional support surface. The dashboard is designed so that object carriers, such as penholders, pipe-holders and other small easily accessible containers, can be hung from it. Under the dashboard there are furniture units with sliding doors, which are extractable and therefore also usable independently. The small table, equipped in this way, is now more similar to a desk. The traditional arrangement of the seats does not invite us to use the car as a place for conversation. *Slipper* offers the possibility of being more comfortable and cosy; the front passengers do not need to turn, since the seats rotate and can face towards the rear bench, creating a circle-like configuration that is ideal for being together, for conversing and for small meetings. The flexible conception of the interior produces the sensation—which has been tested in the field—of travelling shoulder-to-shoulder, travelling together, of the cluster of people in movement.

The *Slipper* car is a vehicle for drivers who live fully the experience of the journey, the sense of movement and the perception of the environment that surrounds him. It is a car that wants to be aware of and kind to the environment, both in movement and standing still.

To fully understand the *Slipper* project, it is necessary to understand the conceptual premises that have generated its philosophy and its basic sentiment.

It is necessary to understand the relationship that a vehicle of this kind wishes to establish with the city. According to Dalisi, the polite car is the path to follow in order to realise a new compatibility between the car and the city.

Dalisi observes that the bursting of the automobile into architecture and into the city has *de facto* transformed its perception and its essence. In contrast, the inverse relationship, that is, the influence of the city on the car, has been very weak. If initially architecture and urban planning seemed to have adapted to the general use of the car, today the city seems to have engaged in a struggle made of obligatory routes, regulated parking, barriers, busy major arteries and limited traffic zones. The contemporary city is therefore comprehensibly forced to defend itself from cars, to contain their presence and invasiveness with barriers, signage system and filters.

'What, then, is the city today? What is the car? If it is true that compatibility is so far yet to be built, then it is the car that has the task of stitching together the fragments: of constructing a city that is diverse due to parts that are physically distant, compacted on each occasion by the dynamics of means of transport; the car creates the bond between the city of groups or individuals, between districts, between different parts of the city, not only from the psychological standpoint, but also on the actual plane of living, working, residing. The Naples-train-Milan-car-aeroplane-London-aeroplane-Milan itinerary can be considered as a unity; the question is: 'How much and in what way must the car or the train compartment take account of this? In other words, is the space of the automobile part of a continuity with the house and the place of employment? Must it have some characteristics of comfort, of the home effect, of the office effect, of the "well furnished corridor" effect? Not only must it have them, but it must also lend itself to a broader use, in the more or less limited and residual times of standing still, or also during movement for those who are not driving; the possibilities of use will give the sense of an interior with a number of functions, albeit minimal.'

¬ *Riccardo Dalisi, Gino Finizio*, Creatività, Design e Management, *Naples: Electa, 2000, 26*

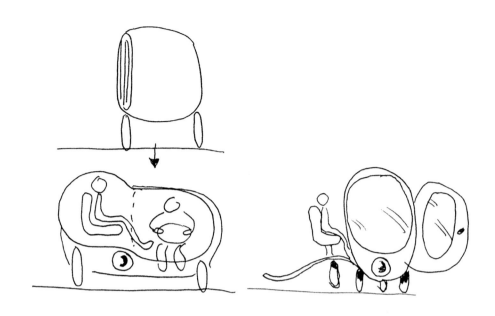

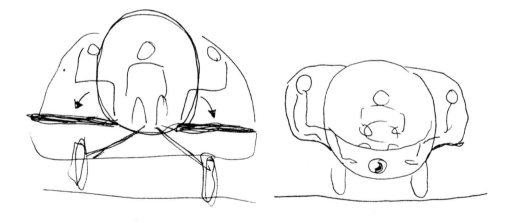

estensione
orizontale.

una cellula e la sua trasformabilità.

The time spent in a car is now more or less inversely proportional to the space travelled: in the past, with a smaller fleet of cars circulating, journey time was directly proportional to the speed of the car and there was no restriction other than the state of the roads and atmospheric conditions. Today, along with those restrictions, others have been added—such as the disproportion between the dimensions of roads and the quantity of cars circulating—paradoxically creating, despite the increase in engine efficiency, an increase in average travelling time. We therefore spend more time in the car even to travel just a few kilometres. The car interior therefore becomes a natural extension of an environment that by definition is intended to be for staying: the house. The body of the car has undergone significant transformations precisely in relation to the emphasis given to the interior space: an example of this is the success that MPVs enjoy today.

The car therefore becomes a small studio apartment that can move: using appropriate materials, it is possible to draw inspiration from the house in order to reflect on and propose innovative solutions.

The personalisation of a product or a product/service is a recognised tendency today in terms of business competitiveness: it coincides with a fragmentation of the market into minimal and transversal sectors for which, ultimately, marketing strategies must give solutions directed at the single individual. In this scenario it is therefore possible to hypothesise various convergences between the semi-finished product, the car interior, and the contribution that artisans can make to the completion of the product: transformability therefore becomes a possible way of localising production and utilising the skills and capacities that are available in a given location.

A further key to interpreting personalisation/transformability concerns the concept of comfort: in this case the adaptability of an interior, not only in an anthropometric or ergonomic, but also a perceptive sense (colours, finishes, sensory stimuli, etc.) becomes a fundamental requirement.

Mario Bellini – Inhabitability

'The car is not immobile when it has stopped, but when it is a place of privation, where the condition of passenger is predominant over that of inhabitant.'

¬ *Mario Bellini*

We are all familiar with the advertising images of automobiles. The dream of other places, landscapes stretching as far as the eye can see, mythical cities. We actually think the car is a means of reaching these places.
Who among us has never had the desire to go out on the motorway and go to find those far-off cities shown in the posters? Off we can go.
This possibility makes us appreciate the car. Alone or in company, we are in control of our lives and the vehicles that transport us.
Yet more often we leave the motorway and wander in search of the place that will save us, that will enable us to abandon that bulky object that is our car. This is the realisation of the dream of forgetting the car and the traffic jam in which we find ourselves, finally free to walk. Unbelievable duality.
It is a formidable paradox that makes this useful object, advanced technology, the desire for liberty, the cause of endless problems, an obstacle to our movements.
We are faced with a double paradox:
– the car, created to allow movement, is in fact becoming increasingly immobile;
– the strong contrast is highlighted between the speed of the vehicle and the immobility inside it (in contrast with the mobility of the horse and rider, with the latter participating in the physical activity of his means of transport).

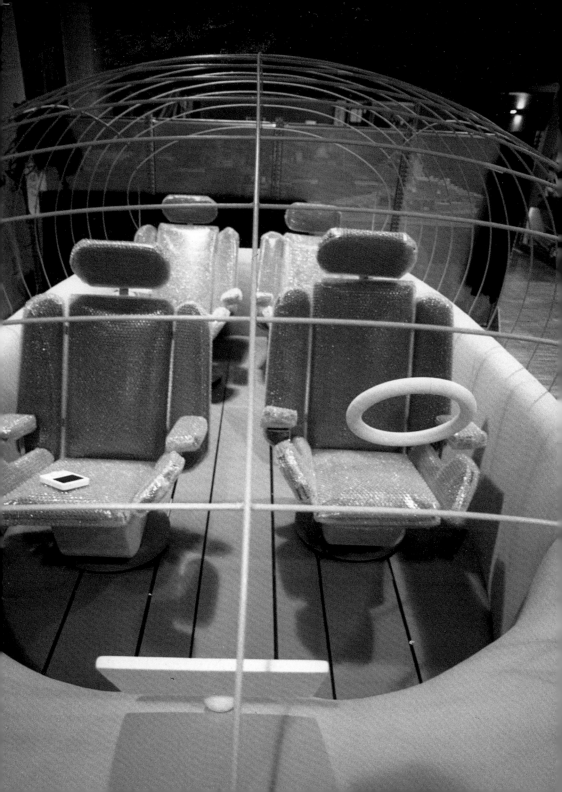

The above considerations have represented the point of departure for the project proposed by Atelier Bellini, developed around a series of closely correlated design themes.

– Inhabiting the mobile space

Mobility has been finally freed from the problems inherent in motion. The space in movement must satisfy the needs associated with contemporary people's activities and expectations: the maximum permeability between interior space and exterior environment, the widespread control over the degree of light penetration and air conditioning.

– The perception of place

Space is a value. The car is designed on the basis of the interior environment. A new principle regulates the relationship between the number of seats and the space available, which is not intended to exhaust the load capacity, whether human or material. The addition of space is not intended as an addition of seats, but as an extension of personal and interpersonal space.

– The metamorphoses

The passengers' space is configured according to modifiable schemes, not necessarily associated with the vectorial sense of transport, but understood as a space in perpetual change. The dashboard is the unit of central control and information no longer only concerns the driver, but also actively involves the other *inhabitants*. The dashboard is therefore no longer an element fixed in time, but participates in the permanent metamorphosis of the interior space and its various functions.

– Sitting and beyond

The car becomes a cell available to host activities independent of motion: relaxation, recreation, work, communication with the interior and the exterior.

– Interactive unit

Besides the various possibilities of regulation and various accessories, in the seats (from the seat proper to the *chaise longue*) the main functional commands will be integrated so as to extend to the maximum the possibilities of movement and the layout of the seats, which are freed from the constraints of position with respect to the interior perimeter.

– The equipped belt

The interior perimeter, freed from the traditional functions, now becomes available to be furnished. The low belt line guarantees the maximum visibility.

The typology of reference for Bellini's project is that of a car that is relatively compact in length, favouring the dimensions of width and height, in order to create a generous interior space. In practice, it is a space in movement that is adaptable, transformable, personalisable, suited for every use, a place of work based on the activity performed, a travelling laboratory for photographers, managers and designers.

Structurally, a stratified supporting platform is hypothesised, with a 'transparent bubble' on top, which identifies the inhabitable space. The platform conceived in this way must house all the mechanical parts—the *power pack*—which, remaining buried inside it, will allow a continuous and regular trafficable surface to be obtained, as well as making space available to hold luggage.

A further hypothesis of development is based on the use of railcar wheels; in this case, the platform will be characterised by a structural boxing along the whole perimeter capable of containing the dimensions of the wheels and suspension system, as well as the various utility spaces. In any case, the space traditionally occupied by the engine is now made available, to the advantage of the interior inhabitability, with the same overall dimensions.

With this project, once again, after the *Kar-a-sutra* project, Mario Bellini transforms the occupants of the car from being simple transported parties into genuine inhabitants of a transformable space in movement.

No longer a 'rocket' to be driven at crazy speed, but an object that is useful when stationary and in movement for a more honest relationship between people and space.

Kann nach oben
die Mitte →
unten
... Hoch stellen
Aufhängung ... auf

Richard Sapper – Elegance

The aim of this study is a car with a physiognomy that is opposed and an alternative to that of the current *Sports Utility Vehicles*, which are imposing, heavy and overbearing. The first design drawings envisage a conceptual prototype with simplicity and functionality as its watchwords: contained dimensions and the gaining of new spaces inside the car.

The return to simplicity is the concept of reference for the project for a new model of car for work and leisure: the reference is to cars such as the *500, 2CV, Mini* and particularly the *Panda*.

It is a vehicle with a light but spacious appearance and with a variable interior; with a clear but not primitive external line.

Every interior element is rendered with the simplicity typical of furnishing products with neat and essential lines, the features that have led to the popularity of Italian design and that characterise our times, as is demonstrated by the success of the trend towards minimalism. In particular, the seats are inspired, for their lightness, essentiality and versatility, by the *Nena* flexible armchair designed by Sapper for B&B Italia and are evidence of the meticulous research work conducted.

Sapper's project rejects the overused reference to military vehicles, but looks with interest at essential and extreme sport vehicles, such as those used to travel in the desert or participate in the Paris-Dakar.

'The idea for this car came about from the Fiat competition at the Akademie der Bildenden Kunste in Stuttgart. One surprising result of this competition was that the students involved in the investigation organised by me in order to begin the project indicated as an ideal type of car for young people, not a sports car, an all-terrain vehicle or race car, but the car that we subsequently made: large, spacious, with a variable interior, to live, to transport everything, to work, to sleep, to make love, where in many projects it was even envisaged to replace manual steering with automatic remote controlled steering. Although I am convinced that those are real needs, I myself would be interested in developing the theme of the car for young people from another angle: that of the elementary but sporty car, on-and off-road, a vehicle that is inspired by the 2CV, R4, Mini, but also the Mini Cooper, Mehari, Panda and Dune Buggy. None of these cars exist anymore and no modern successors exist with the spirit they represented: the pleasure in using them, in driving them, but also enjoying and possessing an automobile with an unconventional appearance, which manifests a personality that many young people want to show. They are the complete opposite of the one made by my students, where this pleasure is denied and replaced by practicality alone. I think—since all young people are not the same—that a significant market niche could well exist for a "free", "pleasure" vehicle, a cross between Panda and BMW, with an image that is the opposite of the Smart car: painted, smooth, multi-coloured, kitsch, a mini-living-room, but with a more "Marlboro" flavour: robust, sporting, natural but elegant; in other words, a car that is more Ralph Lauren than Swatch.

It is clear that such a concept cannot be developed by dividing interior and exterior. The design philosophy of such a car, its physiognomy, should in my view be the opposite of the U.S. Sport Utility Vehicle. That car, which many Americans undoubtedly like a great deal, has a very cutting-edge form, but is not very pleasant: it is large, bulky, heavy, powerful, intrusive, overbearing and extremely ugly. It derives from the jeep, which was beautiful, likeable, because it had a clear and graceful form and was small and simple. All these positive traits were lost in the subsequent transformation: it has been fattened up, made comfortable, had a roof added, then doors, windows, was fattened up further, its clear line softened, complicated, rendered aerodynamic, so to speak, decorated, to create that mongrel that it represents today: the living-room jeep.

The object of this study is a car with an opposite physiognomy: nothing military and no living-room. Instead, a car that draws its features not from all-terrain vehicles, nor from military vehicles, but from sport vehicles, such as the Citroën, such as Dune Buggies.

A vehicle light in appearance, simple in line—sporting but spacious, with a variable interior, but with affordable and elementary means (no Mercedes A type seats), with a clear, but not primitive external

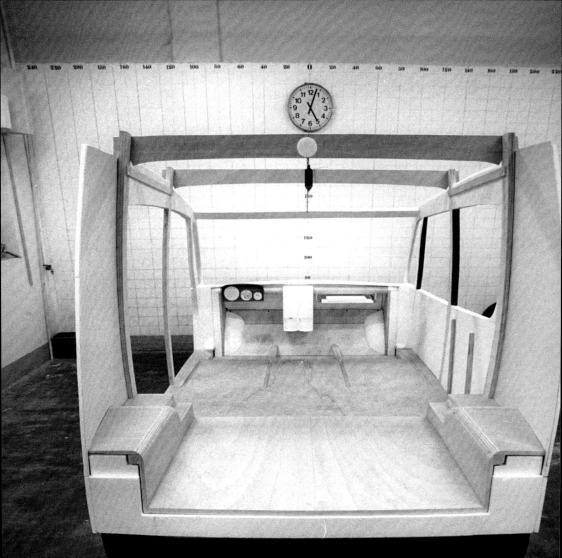

line, that seeks elegance (a car that is not in philosophical opposition to the new Multipla, *but seeks another aesthetic path). The intention is to make the line of the body come about from the interpenetration of two opposing formal concepts: a wholly soft, convex, rounded, aerodynamic element, represented by the face and body of the car with a concave character. All this with the proportions of a road car, but with the possibility of varying the height from the ground considerably. The mechanical way of achieving this aim is to be explored, but I am interested in testing the possibility of not simply increasing the travel of the suspension, but of creating a possibility of raising the body from the suspension system so as to keep the bumpers in a low, or less raised position. This would create an entirely new optical effect, also contributing to safety.'*

¬ Richard Sapper

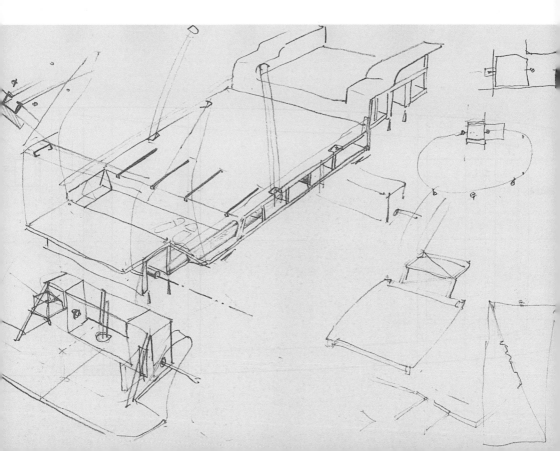

TECNOLOGIS PERCEPITA

Antonio Citterio Architetto
6 - 7 - 00

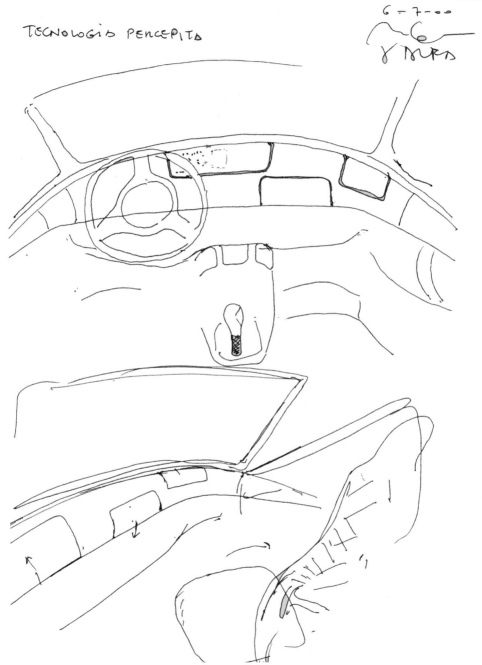

'The new sportiveness is no longer solely the power of the engine or speed, associated with sport and competition, but it is also leisure time, space and comfort. This new relationship with sportiveness defines the designing of car interiors, closely associated with the use of new materials. The transparency of a three-dimensional fabric mesh or the reduction of structural parts to thin magnesium elements change the perception of space, visually extending the reduced interior of the sports vehicle. The field of sports clothing makes available a whole range of innovative synthetic fabrics, which, combined with other materials, represent a response to create a feeling of technology, lightness and sportiveness.

Comfort is no longer a volume but becomes light, and is strongly associated with technology.

The seat is undoubtedly the element where ergonomics and the research into new materials are focused. For instance, the combination of the qualities of tecnogel, which follows a principle of elastic comfort, where it is the gel that adapts naturally to the body in movement, with the performance characteristics offered by the fabric in three-dimensional microstructure, which creates a microclimate between the body and the soft supporting parts. Comfort also derives from the research into new mechanisms and movements to increase the performance characteristics of the seat in order to adapt better to the driver's way of driving and physiognomy. The design of the car interior draws its origins from the wealth of research and from the reduction of the old semantics, with the purpose of arriving at the essence of product sportiveness.'

¬ Antonio Citterio

In a market that is proving to be turbulent and unstable, it is important that the product and the system that gravitates around it manifest a precise identity and distinctive values consistent with the history of the company.

In marketing terms, this means pursuing the positioning of the company, which takes concrete shape in particular in the distinctive characteristics associated with the brand. The strategies of response to the uncertainties of the market pass through a clear and cohesive commitment in keeping the brand policy alive. The company tradition, expressed not only in iconographic terms, but also in the characteristics of fruition (the user's status, behaviour, lifestyle), nevertheless tends towards innovation, in a constant tension between revisiting codes of memory and innovations in line with the characteristics—both tangible and not—of the brand.

An exemplary case is that of Alfa Romeo. The characteristics of products are highly distinctive with respect to other car companies and propose very precise lifestyles. In the collective imagination, also outside Italy, the brand is associated with elite characteristics, with the sharing of prestigious values linked with a concept of quality, comfort, elegance and sportiveness. Alfa Romeo drivers have a very precise image, the characteristics of a club that is sporting and exclusive, of which they are proud to be members.

Until today, in the continuity of the company image, every Alfa Romeo car has in turn proposed this identity code, also affecting the sporting image and the comfort of the interiors with quality materials and finishes, with attention to details and very innovative proposals for the redesigning of certain interior elements. In any case, the design action has always had an aura of quality complementary to it, a certain sportiveness of the proposal.

Indeed, on the Italian markets, and on the international ones where the brand is known and appreciated, this has been one of the elements of the product's competitiveness.

However, other car firms have gradually increased their comfort and attention to detail, improving the effectiveness of a strategy aiming at sporting prestige, leading to a kind of homogenisation of the image of a certain type of car, and with the risk—especially on our market—of blurring the very characteristics that had always distinguished an Alfa Romeo.

Besides the work on the mechanical engineering and the body, important though it may be, what we consider may be seen as an element of characterisation and originality on the current market is the specific work on the car interiors. In particular, returning to the concept of Italian-ness and innovative sportiveness of the product, we wish to stress the possibility of innovating the image of the interiors, referring to that particular context of Italian creativity in the world, furnishings; though having various imitators, these still maintain their own well defined elements of difference, quality and prestige that have made them famous.

Luglio

Michele De Lucchi – Small

Space is a primary asset for people, guaranteeing their well-being and survival. The planet is increasingly populated with people and things, and the size problem has become one of the most important aspects to be considered, imagining a possible positive future.

In this sense we will have to conceive and design, at least for the urban centres, a new minimal, 'small' car, which allows users to move based on actual needs and can be modified, always according to a research into the minimal, based on the various needs and capabilities of users themselves.

To design a *Small* car means designing a minimal space necessary to move people in the urban landscape. The *Small* car is the concept of an 'intermediary car', not a *city car*, nor an all-terrain vehicle, nor a flagship, but rather a means of moving that derives from a utility car based on the model of the *Panda*, the *Twingo*, the *Mini*, the *Mini Moke*, the Citroën *2CV*, the *Mehari* or the *Isetta*. Reading the past, the present and imagining the future, the dimensional future of the car.

To succeed in achieving the minimal possible dimensions, in harmony with the locations of use, for industrial progress that is not punitive for people in their natural lives and takes account of the environment and the cultural heritage.

In all the sectors analysed during this research work—design, furnishings, fashion, mobility—the objects considered have been designed with minimal characteristics and meanings to guarantee the maximum effectiveness and the maximum efficiency.

'The Small *project, implemented during 2000, was launched as a direct result of the experience of the project conducted in 1998, entitled* An extra room. *The concept of space, in fact, still remains central in the current research: rather, this is highly important in the definition of "small" and above all in that of the dimensional parameters of reference. The first question we asked ourselves was: "small", but compared to what? Today there are many small cars already present on the market or else in the phase of presentation, and this theme seems to be of great interest for the car companies, in this historical phase in which traffic problems have intensified and solutions that give a new sense to the "automobile space" have become increasingly necessary.*

We wish to approach the theme from the perspective of architects, which is our own. We want for a moment to seek new points of departure independent from car culture. We want to use the concepts of architectural space applied to the automobile: we are not thinking, that is, of a space devoted to driving, to speed, to the functionality of the automobile tool in a strict sense, but an architectural space, in which movements are not forced by habitual mechanical use, but free, leaving us every flexibility to make more normal, simpler and more uninhibited movements. Often we do not realise how unusual and impractical

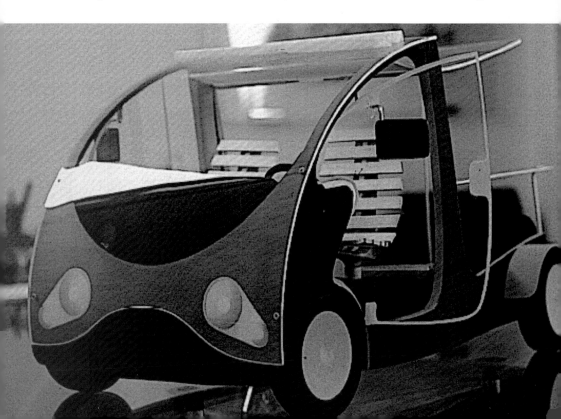

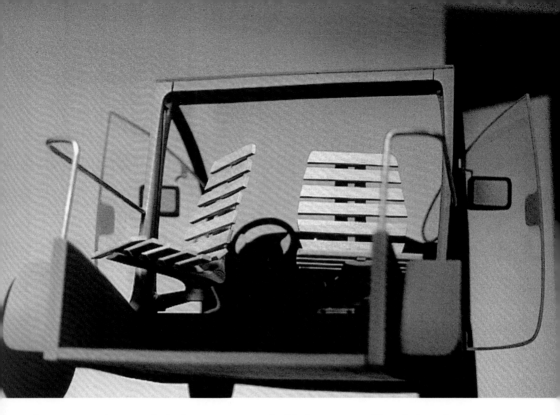

the movements that we make in the car are compared with those we normally make in our houses, offices or anywhere else. The project starts from a prismatic monovolumetric form, without, that is, all the roundings that we are accustomed to seeing in automobiles: the walls and façades are rigidly flat and meet the form of the roof with rigid and precise edges. The realisation of the first models has enabled us to test how extraordinary the amount of space we gain from this is and how airy and free the resulting perception is. Not only that, the image of the car has totally changed and although the trend is to round off edges as much as possible, we achieve a newer, more contemporary and charming image.

The automobile is composed of a wide platform containing the whole part devoted to the engine and movement, to which a dashboard is fixed in the central part that, as well as guaranteeing safety in the event of tipping upside-down, strengthens the roof and sides. In the front part, the roof and sides are defined in a fixed form, while the back part is interchangeable. Four versions are therefore conceivable, which we have initially identified as saloon, van, pick-up and espace. Clearly, many details have yet to be studied, but the launch of the project seems promising to us.'

¬ Michele De Lucchi

easy car

KITA.

'I design thinking about what will be of use.

And I am struck by a feeling of vertigo when I see all the works, one after the other, on display. I cannot manage to give myself a boundary, moving between countries up and down the world, with valid collaborators spread around yet united in a community of views.

As I always repeat, design has no frontiers, like human necessity.

And in fact, just as this is endless, designing for the globe I meet personality after personality.

The past, the present and the future flow for me in a single dimension of spatiality, open onto finalities in discussion, only regulated by a common sensation of balanced space.

With new technologies, today's materials, the changes follow on from each other at a rapid pace under our very eyes, which are looking at a future not yet imagined.

With these thoughts I am pushing forward, of course, in an open path of fertile uncertainties.'

¬ *Toshiyuki Kita*

Easy car is a concept for a city car with reduced dimensions that enables the busy narrow city streets to be penetrated, easily.

The four seats are personalised as though they were a family and, while the front ones are large, flexible and soft, those at the back are reduced and essential: almost lucky seats for a minimal luxury Lancia.

The dashboard is a concentration of ultra-slim technology, a kind of technological samurai sword, incorporating ultra-flat screens and multimedia peripherals according to the refined elegance that also characterises the television equipment designed by Kita for Sharp.

The panels of the car doors are like an accessorised wall: they are composed, in fact, of a series of pockets made of soft materials for carrying objects.

The chromatic fantasy makes the interactive seats even more animated, seeming ready to embrace the occupant.

The panel that covers the car roof internally houses a curious multi-purpose technological diaphragm that brings about a new shared space for passengers.

When he designs, Toshiyuki Kita expresses simplicity and a sense of respect for nature through the use of technology as a resource to create useful products and well-being for people: his aim is to design a product that is simple and suitable for people, in other words a product with a 'soul'.

In order to be chosen, the product must attract, excite; it must have a personality. We are entering the sphere of the emotive, which instinctively acts and selects what fascinates, involves, creates desire, attraction and love, a transfer of sensations, the emotion that strikes you when you are before a work of art, a person, or when you seek the beautiful, the meaning of things: the soul of the object.

A painting, a sculpture, a location, all have a soul; a soul that someone or something has created, giving it form, meaning and the capacity to communicate as a work: an artistic work, a work of art, a unique work.

How can we give a soul to an industrial product when it is multiple, mass-produced, reproducible in so many identical copies? The products must be designed with love and technical skill, using materials and technology, as though they were elements of composition of a work that is then mass-reproduced in industrial environments to become a consumer product.

It is an important creative process conducted by sensitive people who have a soul and are prepared to transfer it to the product they manufacture.

In so doing, the soul of the artist is transmitted into the work and becomes autonomous in the industrial product.

CASA

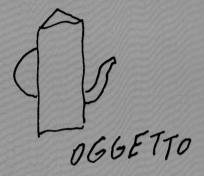

OGGETTO

ABITO

AUTO

Alessandro Mendini – Colour

Some of the images, taken from the research into the creative management of interiors developed at the Atelier Mendini, offer variations on the concepts of harmonious living, Feng Shui, in the dynamic context of the automobile.

The purpose of the investigation is to obtain the maximum emotional response through the adequate use of materials, forms and colours in the car. The result has led to the creation of panels of colours for the car interior and exterior, for use by Fiat Auto Advanced Design. Colour, therefore, becomes a key element for the inhabitability of the car, its visual, psychological and ergonomic comfort.

The colours selected can be integrated into or adapted to suit the locations in which the car moves and have a strong historical reference to the sixties, in which the Fiat *500* was an exceptional protagonist.

INTERNO TUTTO NERO

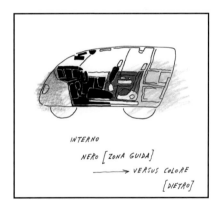

INTERNO

NERO [ZONA GUIDA]
→ VERSUS COLORE
[DIETRO]

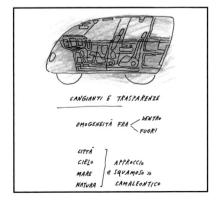

CANGIANTI E TRASPARENZE

OMOGENEITÀ FRA ⟨ DENTRO / FUORI

CITTÀ
CIELO   APPROCCIO
MARE   « SQUAMOSO »
NATURA   CAMALEONTICO

POLVERIZZAZIONE DELL' INTERNO
IN TUTTI I SUOI ELEMENTI

OGNI COMPONENTE
→ HA IL SUO COLORE

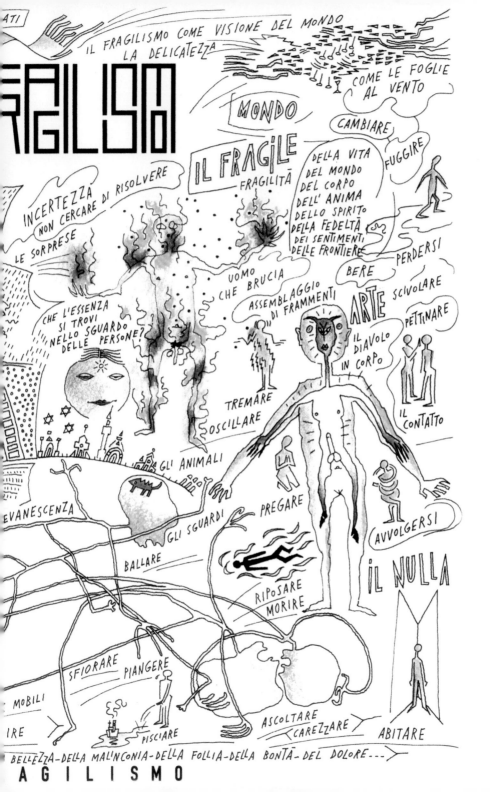

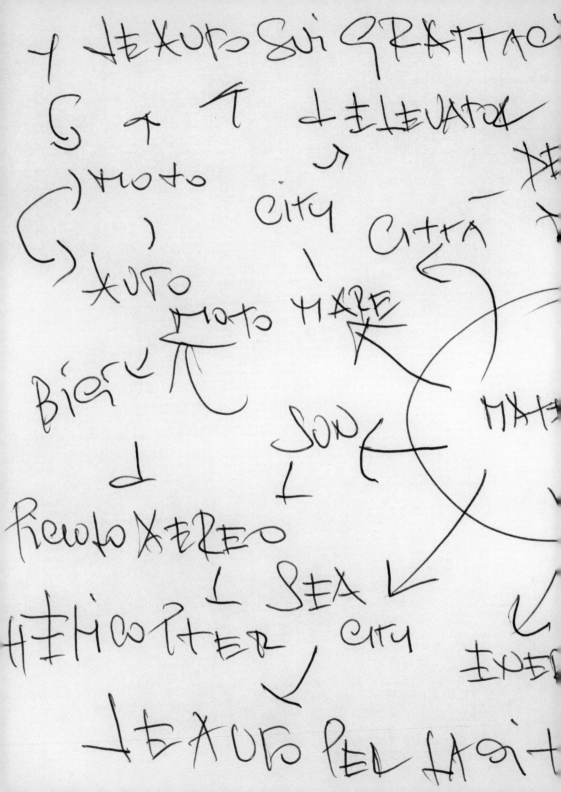

UNA
AUTO INVISIBILE
MARKETING TIME TO MARKET
INNOVATION
DESIGN IDEA
NEW IDEA
RESEARCH
TECHNOLOGY DESIGN
LA CITTÀ DEL MARE
TRANSPORTATION

Jean Nouvel – Distances

When we talk of distances, we think of increasing them or reducing them on the basis of real needs.

The proliferation of means of transport reduces the distances between people and people, but it increases the distances between people and territory. Thus a continuous process is triggered that, on the one hand, fuels technological progress, and on the other hand conditions the balance between species and nature, leaving indelible traces that alter the environment. It is the snake that bites its own tail. These distances, created by man with the use and abuse of means and technologies, require a profound cultural change that can only be realised through a path of creativity, research and design. It is a matter of integrating the design thought of differing and capable intelligences, of revolutionising the system, breaking the traditional aspiration to possess the car to move on to the rational use of the means of transport based on the real needs of movement of people and things, from possession to access to the territory, respecting its cultural heritage.

These are the premises that have guided the creative path developed by Jean Nouvel and fuelled by Fiat Auto Advanced Design. The idea is to create a new model capable of generating intelligent vehicle concepts, capable of living the place without altering its nature. Our cities will probably not change. Paris and Naples will change very little. New architectural installations and variable geometries will characterise them more and more, leaving their essence unchanged. History cannot be modified; it is necessary to live the present and imagine a possible positive future where urban parks will be designed to receive means of transport, realising a greater integration between people and places. Private and public vehicles that live easily in the urban landscape in terms of use, energy, materials and aesthetics. A minimal, transformable, light, transparent means, to enable us to live the colours, the moods of the location. A vertical development of the interior space, made flexible by telescopic mechanisms, increases the relationship between visibility and service space. A solid volume that contains the propulsion system that transmits sensations of force and safety, with on top a light interior that contains the space to live: an invisible boundary with the exterior that amplifies vision and gives a sense of liberty.

To emphasise the concept of immateriality of the interior, intelligent materials are proposed for the car, capable of changing appearance according to the needs of use: transparent plates capable of varying their opacity, to become an interface for the technologies present on board or communicative support on the outer surface. The double platform houses engines, energy and services and is covered by an integrated quilted carpet capable of having various attachments fitted for a differentiated layout of seats, objects and technological accessories; furnishable and personalisable according to users' tastes and requirements. The technological carpet can be manufactured during the production process, according to the buyer's specific requirements: thus the made-to-measure car is realised.

SOFT FLOOR LIKE CHESTERFIELD SOFA
ALUMINIUM FRAME AND PLASTIC BODY
TRANSPARENT DISPLAY
POLISHED ALUMINIUM FRAME
ELECTRICAL ENGINE IN THE WHEELS
FUEL CELL INSIDE THE CHASSIS

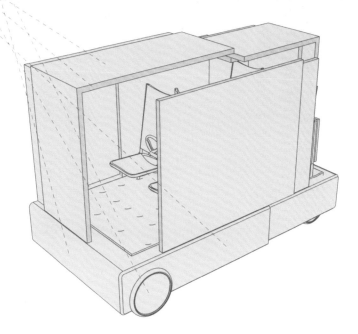

3.3

From Car Design to Transportation Design

The automobile seems to have achieved perfection, a reliable industrial product, a source of earnings for many market sectors, social evolution and freedom of individual movement for work and recreation.

The incessant increase in cars, standing still and in movement, and the energy used to make them circulate, generates traffic and pollution, especially in places with a high urban concentration; this is a phenomenon that has no easy solution, a basic problem that risks undermining the entire system of public and private mobility. A new concept of mobility, where the means designed are used on the basis of the individual's actual needs of movement; no longer cars as status symbols and as social emancipation, but means and systems of mobility that are integrated and connected to a territory that receives them and provides for their possible parking.

In synthesis, a symbiosis between means in movement, people and territory.

During the phase of researching and drafting the book, I never lost sight of the words of architect Ermanno Cressoni, one of the foremost experts in the design and architecture of automobiles and sustainer of the thesis that 'it is not only the automobile that must be revisited, but also the city, which must be organised to receive means of transport'.

I had the pleasure of working and conversing with Ermanno Cressoni, while he was leading a team of designers with a high technical profile, 'authors of the design of the car', people who today still influence the world transportation design scene: Chris Bangle, Pietro Camardella, Peter Davis, Walter De Silva, Wolfgang Egger, Enrico Fumia, Leonardo Fioravanti, Roberto Giolito, Rossella Guasco, Peter Jansen, Flavio Manzoni, Luigi Merlini, Giulia Moselli, Mike Robinson, Andreas Zapatinas, assisted by Margherita Franco and Cinzia Trabucco.

The entire organisational structure, assisted externally by major experts, such as Giorgetto Giugiaro, Sergio Pininfarina, Andrea Pininfarina, Carmelo Di Bartolo, Marco Bonetto and many others, was headed by engineer Nevio Di Giusto (Managing Director of the Fiat Research Centre), one of the leading experts in the world of mobility, means and systems of transport.

In the restructuring of urban centres, disused areas, new housing developments, suitable structures must be designed that are capable of receiving architectures in movement, that strike people precisely through their dynamism, but give life to the city, as the theorists of Futurism had designed and envisaged so well.

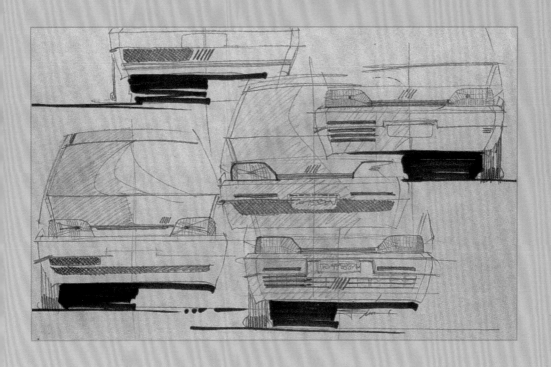

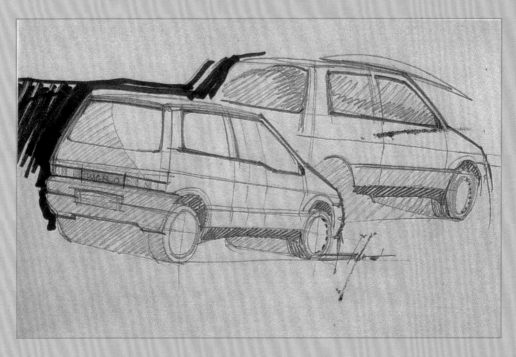

Ermanno Cressoni

'It is necessary to "mix races", because for far too long there have been designers of automobiles, of appliances, of spoons, of cities, each defending their own positions.

It is necessary to interrelate the projects and the various experiences of other ways of doing design.

At times it is correct to give solutions to meet users' demands, at other times to anticipate them.

In some cases the need is latent and we interpret it, even if this phenomenon is more associated with short timescales.

If we ask those who have a design culture: "How do you use the car?", the answer a comment on the interior, on how to experience it and not how to move it.

The car is a kind of studio apartment that can be moved. It therefore has four dimensions.

The materials are different from those of furnishing, because the space is lived in a much more intense and spartan manner. If we observe the transformation of automobile forms, we have moved on from a long bonnet, the symbol of mechanical power, to an MPV, which represents the negation of the engine in favour of the inhabited space.

Convenience is the "new frontier", and cars will be increasingly designed from the inside out, and not vice versa.'

¬ Ermanno Cressoni

Innovative Thought

'...Yes, modern architecture is young architecture—the joy of youth must bring it. The love of youth, eternal youth must develop and keep it. You must see this architecture as wise, but not so much as wise as sensible and wistful, nor anymore scientific than sentient, nor so much resembling a flying machine as a masterpiece of the imagination. And yet, man made environment is the truest, most characteristic of all human records. Let a man build and you have him. You may not have all he is, but certainly he is what you have.'

¬ *Frank Lloyd Wright, in* Collected Writings, *Ed. Bruce Brooks Pfeiffer*

Man expresses his thoughts by communicating and acting with consistent behaviour; when the sphere of action is study, research, design and culture, these thoughts evolve constructively, thus producing a novel value, an original thought, an innovative thought.

Frank Lloyd Wright is one of the architects who have most produced innovation in thought and design; this is visible in his every gesture. His behaviour in life and work is exemplary and leaves a solid cultural inheritance to contemporary architecture and to the relationship that this must have with the nature that surrounds it.

Broadacre city (1934–58), Frank Lloyd Wright's city-territory, proposes the urbanisation of the whole territory by assigning one acre of land (4,000 square metres) to each inhabitant. This is an ideal city that is developed horizontally and supersedes at root the city-country opposition in a landscape continuum in which every residence is surrounded by vegetation. It is an innovative urban planning vision that gives supreme value to the freedom of the individual, firmly supported by progress in the means of communication and transport: telephone, automobile and futuristic flying machines. Wright was the first to understand the effects of the car on patterns of urban growth. Broadacre City is a plan for the occupation of the territory that is in opposition to the casual and uncontrolled expansion of the city and the periphery. Way ahead of his time the US master architect had sensed the possible consequences of the advent of the automobile, the need for a complete integration of artificial and natural environments, the urgent requirement to design housing schemes that would be complementary to nature and the landscape, which at the same time would be open to the new possibilities offered by technology.

Broadacre City proposes an idea of the city that is very different from Le Corbusier's Ville Radieuse. Nevertheless, in both projects the car fulfils a key role for the movements of individuals. This role, which has become a reality in a contemporary city that today is no longer capable of bearing it due to the effects of traffic that is out-of-control.

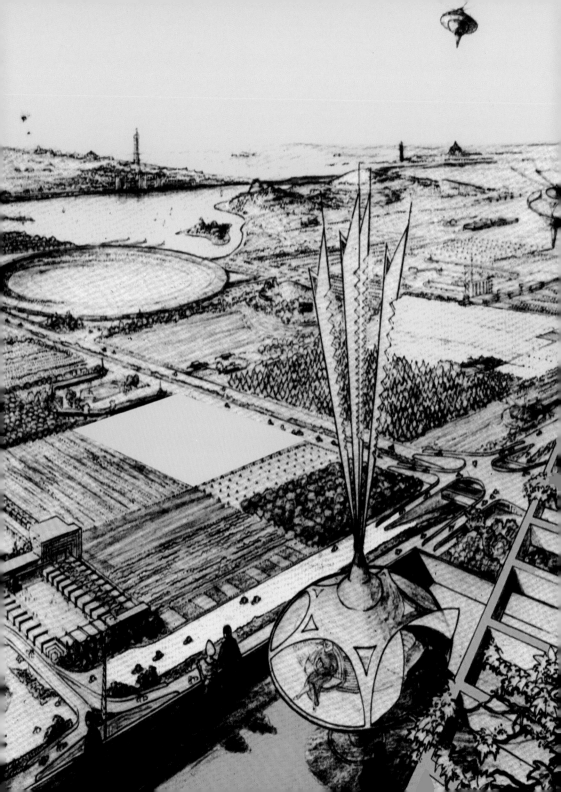

Design for Innovation in Enterprise

After years of research and meetings with architects, designers and industrialists on the theme of architecture and mobility, tradition and innovation, there appears to be an even clearer need to press on with a project programme that encourages progress without punishing the environment. Technology must be used wisely, avoiding useless abuses that make people the victims of an evolution that their own intelligence produces. Architecture and mobility express the social, economic and industrial culture of our age, yet we have not yet succeeded in finding a formula that can integrate the whole road system in an organic and efficient way such as to guarantee clean air and the conservation of the social and cultural patrimony of our planet. Tradition is set in opposition to innovation; there is a fear of surrendering acquired values to follow uncertain paths; there is defence of the normal, the classic, the manageable and there is concentration on the recovery of memory due to uncertainty and rejection of the new. According to the defenders of tradition, innovation unhinges the acquired system, conservation is tranquillity gained. What, then, are the scales, the measurements? What is the system that makes us decide whether it is right or not right to change? How can we give a response to the eternal question, to the Hamletic doubt that torments us: to change or not to change, tradition or innovation? Progress draws strength from the conquests of medicine, from the increase in average lifespans, from the reduction of distances and improvements in communication. Can all these benefits make us forget the negative aspects that progress itself produces? To seek a different, alternative response, we have chosen to analyse the pragmatic world of industrial enterprise and particularly the path of development of 3M, one of the companies that have most influenced change. Indeed, the company has over a century of history behind it; it is the same age as modern architecture, the automobile, cinema and industrial innovation. 3M, whose inventions have accompanied the progress of our age in so many fields, can give a response to our alternative questioning. The longevity of 3M depends on their undisputed capacity to make innovative products, but also to translate technological discoveries into tools and applications that are truly useful for people. A company is a living, growing organism, generating new products that are welcomed by the market of reference. The basis of their process of evolution is constantly targeted research into specific sectors that can create value and economic benefits. This basic philosophy has been applied by 3M for more than a hundred years and this has enabled them to maintain their leadership in many market sectors and to merit the title of an outstanding company for their enterprise and products. The intrinsic capacity of the well known US multinational to update their structure regularly and to expand effectively in the countries with the highest rate of development makes the company resistant and able to ride the wave of changes under way. The company organisation is capable of overcoming the obstacles it encounters, deriving from sudden economic and scenario changes, eliminating dead ends and dry branches with a political effectiveness of management control. Speed of adaptation to emerging market situations is a prerogative of a few excellent companies that manage to remain on the crest of the wave. The engine of resources, deriving from the constant research that 3M carries out, is such as to guarantee the development of the company over time. An effective, flexible method that has rarely known economic failure, characterised by evolved marketing, operational plans, group spirit, logistics, management control, profit centres, factors that decrease business risk and favour the development of the company in harmony with nature.

What are the risk factors to be faced for the immediate future? What are the key points to be consolidated? What strategies can reduce risk in a turbulent market, blighted by dumping policies continually practised by emerging countries? Can research, constant updating, flexibility and orientation towards design mean a solution to possible problems of growth? 3M, already attentive to research and innovation, is developing an intelligent policy of receptiveness to design that can guarantee the maintenance of leadership. Design is a strategic business factor; research feeds innovation; materials guarantee quality; design moulds form and highlights the function of the product, which becomes recognisable and attractive.' What business strategy has enabled 3M to remain on the crest of the wave in a hundred years of activity? What is their behaviour with respect to tradition and innovation? An initial response is inherent in the history of the company and is legible in the long list of products and inventions that have made innovation a key value over the course of a century. The company has demonstrated not only that it knows how to conquer the leadership in the markets where it is committed, but also that it is able to create new ones, thanks to newly 'invented' products, in which it has the greatest expertise. The parallel development of numerous technological platforms has generated an extreme differentiation. 3M market over 50,000 products, a myriad of materials and components on which the performance and quality of complex finished products depend. Although 3M is present in many 'technical' sectors, the great renown of the brand is also associated with certain tools and items that are very commonly used, such as sandpaper, Scotch adhesive tape, Post-it notes, the retro-reflective materials used for road signage, OLF film (optical lighting film), Scotch Brite, to name just a few of the major inventions produced by the company. According to 3M, innovating means above all inventing new materials and improving the performance of the existing ones. Thus we understand the importance the company attributes to technological research, in which it invests conspicuous financial and human resources. The study of materials proceeds in step with the investigation into possible applications to take advantage of their performance characteristics and intrinsic qualities. The development of a line of original research may even last decades and generate a large number of products. The research into adhesive materials, for example, initially led to the creation of Scotch, then to the Post-it note and more recently to a vast range of films with which it is possible to improve the resistance of glass, but also to decorate a wall or a means of transport. This is a strategic choice that allows the company to concentrate major resources on research and innovation. 3M has a solid relationship with art, which is the source of inspiration behind their operational programmes. The graphic order introduced by Piet Mondrian for the organisation of the company's divisions and products is the demonstration of this relationship, which is legible in all the 3M literature. The 3M brand designed by the Great Master in 1960 is an indelible sign that leaves a profound mark on the history of modern industry. The unmistakable matrix stamped on the cover of the *1968 Annual Report 3M*, which I collected from the company headquarters in St. Paul in Minnesota in that year, is further confirmation that art survives in industrial enterprise.

Art, design, organisation, ecology, transparency, ethical behaviour: these are dominant and irreplaceable factors for the success of contemporary companies. 3M provides a concrete example of this transparent action that blends different cultures in a sole objective tending towards economic and social progress.

270

3M
COMPANY

VERITI
2004

Scotchprint

1991

RESEARC

Oltt 1988

DESIG

POST-it 1980

APPLICAT

Gino Finizio

DESIGN

1972

NOMAD

MATE

1968

Post-it® 3M
Premio Industrial Design 1990

LIGHTWATER

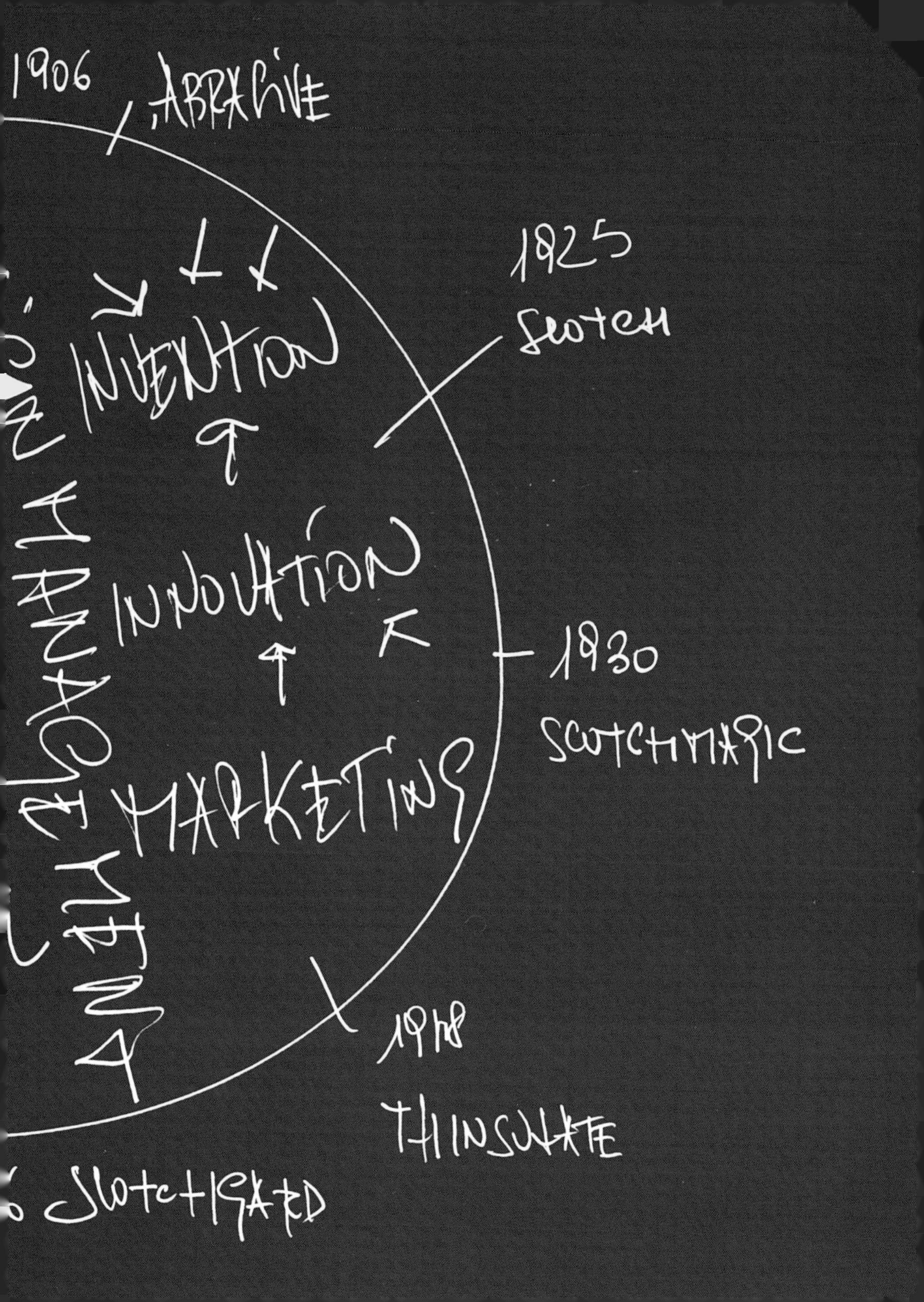

1906 , ABRASIVE

1925
SCOTCH

INVENTION
&

INNOVATION
&

1930
SCOTCHMAGIC

MARKETING

MANAGEMENT

1948
THINSULATE

SCOTCHGARD

Design around the Idea

How do the 'inventions' of 3M come about?

Creativity needs a fertile terrain, a place capable of valuing it with concrete choices, a company attentive to its own workforce that holds individual scientific and creative qualities in the maximum consideration. It is for this reason that in 3M, under their contracts, each employee is free to devote 15% of their time to personal projects, insights, experimentations, with the possibility of using the company's laboratories and instruments in total freedom. This approach has made possible, for example, the creation of famous and ingenious products such as Post-it notes, around the 'invention' of which a vast literature has emerged. The initial idea dates back to 1968, when Spencer Silver, a 3M researcher, discovered a new adhesive that only stuck lightly to surfaces and could be easily removed and repositioned. Ten years went by before his colleague Art Fry found a practical application for this. An insight that came about from a passion for singing prompted him to make some bookmarks for pages of musical score. The chronicles do not always report, however, that two years of research were needed to transform the initial idea into a product concept, nor that the company conducted numerous trials before introducing Post-its definitively on the market in 1980. Over 25 years later, these notes have become a constant presence in every office and perhaps even provided a possible answer to our initial question, an example of technology at the service of people. The policy of innovation is therefore read in the products, but also in the whole company approach, which takes creativity as a resource to be managed with method. Naturally, the selection of the ideas to be developed takes place according to rigorous criteria of cost-benefit analysis to respond to preset objectives. There is no internal conflict here, but collaboration to improve the level of quality pursued through evolved processes of optimisation. 'The company is a living organ that is born, grows, proliferates and is refreshed to remain in step with the times. Its lifeblood is innovation; research feeds its growth and design forges its identity. Design is an indelible sign, a thin thread that runs from product to product to make them different, recognisable, desirable, unique and inimitable.

Design generates the difference that determines success.

A company that does not update will slowly fade until it naturally dies: it is extinguished through inertia.'

In the initial analysis it might seem that the best 3M products are utensils without 'design', above all when they are materials that perform a service (Scotch tape) or components of other products (Thinsulate).

What role does design have? Probably marginal, if understood in the meaning that links the production of an industrial object with the design work that enriches it with an aesthetic quotient. But this would be a vision that is limiting for the role of 'design', a discipline that in fact lends itself to multiple variations.

At this moment 3M's strong interest in design arrives as a response to a wider need, on the one hand as a synonym for the propensity for innovation, on the other as an instrument to be receptive to the demands of consumers and for the development of new applications.

The study of the dispensers for adhesive tape is a clear example of this strategy. In the same way, the idea of selling the pre-cut Scotch strips (1997) is another case of easy use of the product-material.

3M, a leader in materials, has launched a further process of receptiveness to design that will also make the company a leader in this field, like Sony, Apple and Philips, constructing an identity that is common to all products, even if they belong to different commodity sectors.

The new strategic centrality of design reinforced the 'traditional' values of 3M, technological innovation and the soundness of the brand. Design will help technology to be useful, affordable and desirable at the same time. The brand will not only be synonymous with reliability, but a point of reference for consumers, providing a competitive advantage for the company.

An important step in this direction was the opening of the 3M Design Center in 2002. Milan has been selected as the venue to underline the company's closeness to the world of fashion and design, where items are catalysed, produced and relaunched all over the world. The design centre works at the same time with a team inside the company and with designers from Italy and abroad who are called upon on each occasion to handle specific projects. From the creativity and expertise of each, through constant dialogue, the company has filtered and co-ordinated the ideas that are most consistent with the development of a programme with broader scope.

Design may favour the development of enterprise, the cohesiveness of projects; the choice of suitable materials and technologies can lead to important processes of economic and social evolution of the business and market system.

The consumer becomes the customer and a committed friend of the company; the products are a natural choice of those who use them.

The objects are publicised by word of mouth among the increasing numbers of fans of the brand: this is a sort of social circle in movement, where people feel like members of a single group that represents their way of being, thinking and communicating. This is a less aggressive form of marketing that seeks the permission of its customer friends to supply them with what they want and how much they want; a new philosophy of the company and market relationship that blends Eastern and Western origins due to the need people have not to feel like the instruments of advertising campaigns and business strategies.

Design with the aid of marketing aims to satisfy customers with products that are useful, ecological and ergonomic; real objects designed for people and their well-being. A new era, in short, where it is the real and not the ephemeral that is sold. In this context, companies are guarantors of the services provided without false purposes and with industrial profits and not short-term speculative ones.

The recent products presented by 3M after the settling of the Design Centre in Milan represent this emerging philosophy. The materials and the technology are moulded through the design to become widely distributed objects for a new culture of use and not of abuse.

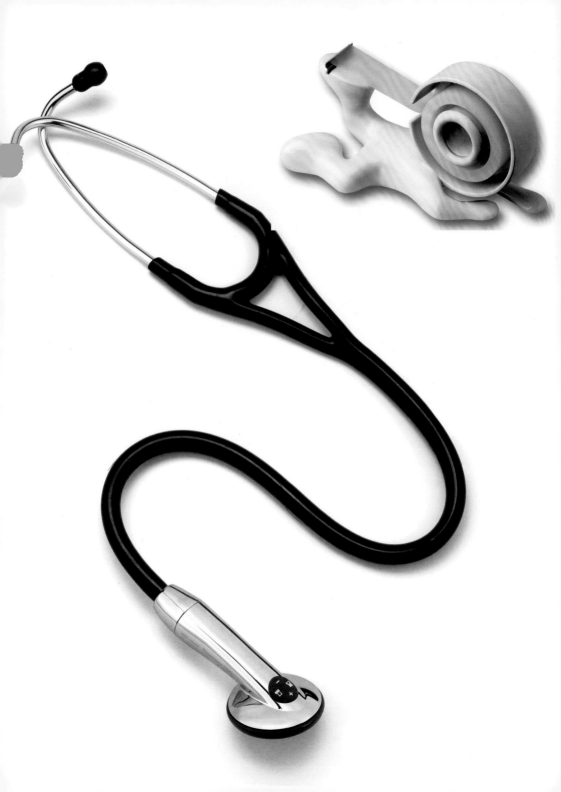

Architectures in Movement: Travelling Cities

The size problem does not concern static central and peripheral architectures alone.

Urban centres with a high population concentration are places often characterised by building speculation, which creates 'concrete boxes' inhabited by disparate populations living at the bounds of decency, contemporary ghettos, which seem extraneous to the social and technological evolution that marks the path of contemporary civilisation. The optimum distribution of spaces concerns all architectures in movement; the ways of building them, living in them and using them are signs of emancipation of the country that produces them. The materials employed in the designing of vehicles contribute to innovating the mobility system, making it more suited to our times. A sphere of particular interest is the naval environment, where the growth of the sector enables a new philosophy to be outlined for the evolved designing of vessels.

Leaving aside small boats and pleasure crafts, where the space-person ratio is satisfied on the basis of the purchasers' specific requirements, it is appropriate to focus on the spaces in ships of large dimensions to study their architecture, design and the quality of the services provided. The design of the most advanced sectors of Italian production may suggest the possible innovations in a strategic sector such as that of cruise ships. The architecture project for the interiors, particularly the cabins, is interesting and opportune to implement a process of greater industrialisation of the furnishing product, which until now has been built on a hand crafted basis. Naval architectures, full-blown floating cities, not afflicted by vehicle traffic, must envisage an optimum space/person ratio that must be innovated constantly and conveyed towards a greater integration between engineering, naval layout design and the safety of on-board services. It is a matter of producing innovation in the individual components of the project in order to increase the overall value of the product. The idea of combining naval engineering culture with the culture of materials and design is an experience that is undoubtedly interesting and must be mentioned and nourished.

The 'naval cabin' design concept developed in 2006 by 3M (Mario Galfetti, Sergio De Masi, Roberto Tarallo), Fincantieri (Piercirpiano Rollo, Marco Badaracco, Luigi Pastorino, Antonello Gamaleri, Vittorino Giolo) and Gino Finizio Design Management (Gino Finizio, Lorenzo Facchini, Claudio Formicola, Roberto Rovetta, Marcello Sebis, Alessandro Villa) is a valid example of the design integration between 'client and supplier' and designer that deserves to be expressed. An example of Italian creativity applied with broad scope, which is innovative in method, in the approach to business, as well as in the project proposals. It has been a matter of innovating the 'cabin' product starting from its tradition without neglecting its values, but adapting the entire system to suit a concept of evolution that takes account of the variables in scenario on the cultural, social and evolutionary plane of people. Such a product aims to provide service and efficiency in every location, even in unpredictable emergency situations. The specialistic characterisation of naval cabins has prompted us to reflect on how to develop an effective project that respects precise and far from negligible prerequisites, such as the maximum lightness, the highest resistance to fire and the safety of passengers and crew.

Observations on the state of the art and meetings with experts highlighted a whole series of constraints, critical elements for the construction of a comfortable inhabitable space, which can be summarised as:

– dimensions reduced to a minimum;

– frequent absence of natural lighting;

– high density of people in relation to the space available;

– presence of noise and vibrations;

– prolonged stays of personnel on board.

The analysis of the relationship between the cabin and the ship as a whole is of assistance in the identification of new lines for the designing of a new idea of an inhabitable naval cell. The great cruise ships offer a lifestyle that makes them increasingly similar to a floating city. The space of the cabin, of the places devoted to stays on board, cannot be completely detached from the perception of being part of a large means of transport in movement over the boundless surface of the sea. The cabin is an important element of evaluation of the perceived quality and comfort of a ship. The furnishings must be in step with styles of life and behaviour, but at the same time it is necessary to optimise production timescales and processes. Installation on board is one of the major costs and difficulties, also in terms of the management of the order. The objective of the project is to transfer the largest possible number of operations onto land, into the workshop, in order to arrive at an almost finished product, which is ready to be placed on board and 'hooked up' to the network of installations. The activity of the project group culminated in the realisation of an actual scale mock-up, fitted out in the 3M headquarters in Segrate, to allow the actual perception of the environment, as well as the application of the materials actually expected to be used on board ship. The model has been the object of various subsequent updates, to improve the solutions at a high technological level and to demonstrate the possibilities of personalising the project on the basis of the requirements of potential customers. An experimental laboratory where the 3M experience has been concentrated in the field of adhesive materials, in lighting techniques, in the coverings of surfaces, in safety devices, in the products and techniques for wiring, in new materials. The action of the integrated design group has taken account of the business demands and strong points of both Fincantieri and 3M in order to develop—autonomously—a design concept of a naval cabin evolving towards the optimisation of the person-space ratio and functionality combined with perceivable technology.

Basic table of 3M materials for Fincantieri cabin model							
FiberGlass tube			**Di-NOC**			**RESIN**	
TYPE	*Quantity*	*Dimension*	*Material*		*Quantity*	Floor:	Colorquartz 7133
tubes	12	cm 198					
tubes	28	cm 26	roof:	PS 957	25 m		
tubes	16	cm 154	wall:	FE 806	50 m		
tubes	3	cm 100	wall:	PS 141	25 m		
tubes	2	cm 193	wall:	PS 917	25 m		
tubes	1	cm 141	wall:	PS 910	25 m		
joints	60	45°	tube:	ME 604	25 m		
joints	64	90°					

Static Architectures and Dynamic Architectures

During the creative process for the drafting of the book we have on many occasions indicated the symbiosis existing between static forms and forms in movement, between means of transport and urban infrastructures. Static architectures tend to stretch out into the air that surrounds them, looking for new harmonious forms that are projected into space with liberty, forming avant-garde architectural expression. The conquest is towards the sky, the countryside, the desert, the rivers, the forest, the open sea: a movement that goes towards nature. At the same time, dynamic architectures, cars, trains, planes and other means of transport, take on solid forms, similar to those of static volumes, to conquer secure energy to be transferred to the passengers, who become inhabitants of modern, comfortable new locations.

These technically advanced environments are similar to residences and offices, though remaining intelligent mobile projected forms in harmony with the places that receive them and capable of communicating with each other and with central and peripheral infrastructures.

The emerging technologies, moulded by experienced hands and creative minds, allow the development of new evolved forms and habitats that are ever more functional and innovative.

Contemporary architectural planning takes account of the demands of the people in movement, of the new nomadic culture that, during the wanderings of holiday-makers, commuters and businesspeople, seeks active comfort to suit the times. The cities of the sea seem to be most sought-after by people who want to live in harmony with nature and to breathe fresh, clean air, a primary resource for the survival of the species that populate our planet.

Cruise ships, real floating cities, seem to be favoured by nomadic peoples who seek tranquil places without traffic and pollution and want to sail with the visual comfort of landscapes without confines or limits attainable by the human eye, enchanted places to remember and tell about as through a fantastic dream, one often unrepeatable in one person's lifespan.

What is the dream?

A house projected towards the sea, resting on the crest of a hill, nourished with greenery, breathing clean air and intoxicated by the song of the sea: a harmony of songs and sounds that knows no limits to its repertoire. A house always ready to set sail, though remaining soundly anchored to and attracted by terra firma, with no place more enchanting and exclusive to be found on the vast sea map as the one where Casa Malaparte stands.

Can we all consume the dream?

No, but we can pretend and organise with due determination a progress in step with the times, where it is people who guide their destiny as inhabitants of the earth, who look at the universe and are reflected in its mysterious immensity.

286

Photography

A concept expressed out loud and clearly is not easily replaceable with other systems and means of communication. The direct oratorical exposition, the elegant word, assisted by the sounds and gestures of skilled speakers, may render communication and understanding highly effective.

Sometimes the traditional way of disseminating one's own thought is not sufficient to impress upon the minds of those who listen what one wishes to transmit.

The transcription of the theme expressed in an organised and legible manner succeeds more easily in disseminating concepts, which can be analysed, read and reread until the sense of the thought transmitted is perceived.

Writing, plus the design, makes each concept legible and the graphic representations can contribute to disseminating the entire communication project.

Works of art—architecture, sculpture, painting and every artistic work—do not require comments to accompany them: it is the work itself that transmits what is expressed by the author to those who know how to interpret it.

In order to be complete, a book needs written text, designs, figures and graphic editing, but in order to transfer the reality of facts, it needs to represent this through photography.

The art of this century is communication; the photograph is the synthesis that disseminates its reality.

The photograph is expressive art that, if produced by artists who know how to grasp the instant, the magical moment that does not return, becomes an irreplaceable precious asset.

In writing *Architettura & mobilità. Tradizione e innovazione* I have worked alongside my son Gianpaolo, who has been well able to 'grasp the instant', trapping the major players in the book, standing still and in movement, and even more my thought, in magical photographs.

Mandra

Vivere su un'isola.
Passeggiare lontano dai rumori della città,
respirare aria pura, guardare il mare,
cancellare tutti i pensieri con l'onda che viene e che va.
Non parlare, farsi spiegare dai pesci, muovendo solo le labbra,
come fanno sotto l'acqua a parlare.
Cala la sera:
mi manca la città, la luce, l'energia che pulsa.
Penso ai miei amici del progetto, comincio a nuotare verso la terra ferma
per unirmi a loro e disegnare una nuova era, dove il progresso avanza
di pari passo con la natura.

To live on an island,
To walk far away from the noises of the city,
To breathe pure air, to look at the sea,
To cancel out all thoughts with the wave that comes and goes.
Not to speak, to be explained by the fish, moving only your lips,
As they speak under the water.
The evening falls:
I miss the city, the light, the pulsating energy.
I think about my friends in the project, I start to swim towards terra firma,
To join them and design a new era, where progress advances
In step with nature.

Captions

Bibliography

Ambasz, E., *Italy: The New Domestic Landscape*, Florence: Centro Di, 1972.

G. Anceschi (ed.), *Il progetto delle interfacce*, Milan: Domus Academy Edizioni, 1993.

Benevolo, L., *Storia dell'architettura moderna*, Rome–Bari: Laterza, 1987.

Bellucci, A., *L'automobile italiana*, Bari: Laterza, 1984.

Boissière, O., *Jean Nouvel*, Paris: Terrail, 1996.

Bonsiepe, G., *Dall'oggetto all'interfaccia*, Milan: Feltrinelli, 1995.

Brooks Pfeiffer, B., *Frank Lloyd Wright*, Cologne: Taschen, 1991.

Buchanan, P., *Renzo Piano. L'opera completa del Renzo Piano Building Workshop*, vol. II, Turin: Umberto Allemandi & C., 1996.

Cerri, P., and Nicolin, P., *Le Corbusier. Verso una architettura*, Milan: Longanesi & C., 2002.

Dal Co, F., Foster, K.W., Soutter, A.H., *Frank O. Gehry. Tutte le opere*, Milan: Electa, 2003.

Dalisi, R., and Finizio, G., *Creatività, Design e Management. Percorsi nella cultura del progetto*, Naples: Electa, 2000.

Eminente, G., *Il design industriale nelle strategie di mercato*, Milan: Etaslibri, 1991.

Finizio, G., *Design management, gestire l'idea*, Milan: Skira, 2002.

Frateili, E., *Continuità e trasformazione. Una storia del disegno industriale italiano – 1928/1988*, Milan: Alberto Greco Editore, 1989.

Godet, M., *Scenari e gestione strategica*, Rome: Ipsoa, 1990.

Hosoe, I., Marinelli, A., Sias, R., *Playoffice*, Tokyo: G.C. Press Co., 1991.

Koolhaas, R., *S, M, L, XL*, Rotterdam: The Monacelli Press, 1995, 130.

Koudate, A., *Il management della progettazione*, Turin: Isedi Petrini editore, 1991.

Le Corbusier, *Urbanistica*, Milan: Il Saggiatore, 1967.

J. Lucan (ed.), *Le Corbusier Enciclopedia*, Milan: Electa, 1988 (volume published on the occasion of the exhibition *The Le Corbusier Adventure*).

Lorenz, C., *Dimensione design. L'arma vincente della competizione globale*, Milan: Franco Angeli, 1990.

Mandrelli, D., *Massimiliano Fuksas (Frames)*, Barcelona: Actar Editorial, 2001.

L. Parmesani (ed.), *Alessandro Mendini. Scritti*, Milan: Skira, 2003.

Momo, P., and Zucchelli, F., *Design to success. Come concepire e progettare prodotti vincenti*, Turin: ISEDI, 1997.

Morace, F., *Controtendenze. Una nuova cultura del consumo*, Milan: Domus Academy ed., 1990.

Morace, F., *Metatendenze*, Piacenza: Sperling & Kupfer Editori, 1996.

Morace, F., *PreVisioni e PreSentimenti*, Piacenza: Sperling & Kupfer Editori, 2000. Morgan, C.L., *Starck*, Milan: Rizzoli, 1999.

Morgan, C.L., *Marc Newson*, Milan: Skira, 2002.

Morphosis. Buildings and projects, essays by Cook, P., Rand, G., New York: Rizzoli International Publications, 1989.

Morphosis. Buildings and projects. 1989-92, introduction by Weinstein, R., New York: Rizzoli International Publications, 1994.

Pevsner, N., Fleming, J., and Honour, H., *Dizionario di architettura*, Turin: Einaudi, 1981.

Rambert, F., *Massimiliano Fuksas*, Paris: Editions du regard, 1997.

Richard Sapper design, Cologne: Museum für Angewandte Kunst, 1993.

Sort, J.J., *Metropolitan networks*, Barcelona: Editorial Gustavo Gili, 2005.

Starck, London: Taschen, 1999.

Starck, P., *Starck*, London: Taschen, 2000.

Storia del disegno industriale. 1851-1918. Il grande emporio del mondo, Milan: Electa, 1990.

Tafuri, M., and Dal Co, F., *Architettura contemporanea*, Milan: Electa, 1992.

Turinetto, M., *Automobile. Glossario dello stile*, Vimodrone: Giorgio Nada editore, 2000.

Tutte le Fiat, Rozzano: Editoriale Domus, 2001.

Venturi, R., *Complessità e contraddizioni nell'architettura*, Bari: Edizioni Dedalo, 1991.

Magazines

Bellini, M., 'Architettura e design: considerazioni', *Domus*, 675, 1986.

Branzi, A., 'Il sopravvento della logica fuzzy', *Domus*, 800, 1998.

Burckhardt, F., 'Editoriale', *Domus*, 792, 1997.

Burckhardt, L., 'Maggese come contesto', *Domus*, 784, 1996.

Cardani, E., 'Tolosa. Il Centro congressi Compans Caffarelli', in *L'Arca Plus*, 01.

Chaslin, F., 'Il futuro sarà fatto di cambiamento', *Domus*, 800, 1998.

Diaz Moreno, C., and García Grinda, E., 'A conversation with Jean Nouvel', *El Croquis*, 2002, 112–13.

Finizio, G., 'Cambiamo aria', *Quattroruote*, 592, February 2005.

Finizio, G., 'Dal possesso al noleggio', *Noleggio*, October 2003.

Finizio, G., 'Mario Bellini e il design' (interview with M. Bellini), *Ottagono*, 117, December 1995–February 1996.

Finizio, G., 'Qualificare la forma' (interview with R. Dalisi), *Ottagono*, 110, March 1994.

Finizio, G., 'Prodotti senza tempo', *Progettare*, 282, October 2004.

Finizio, G., 'Progettista e advanced designer', *Progettare*, 287, March 2005.

Finizio, G., 'Progettista, designer', *Progettare*, 235, June 2000.

Finizio, G., 'Un futuro da inventare' (interview), *Quattroruote*, 578, December 2003.

Finizio, G., and Kita, T., 'Limite e moltitudine: la progettazione', *AR2*, 2, 2004.

Lovegrove, R., 'Gaia fotovoltaica', *Domus*, 800, 1998, 80.

Mendini, A., 'Dalla sintesi alla contaminazione delle arti', *Domus*, 794, 1997.

Moore, R., 'Ristrutturazione di palazzo a Budapest', *Domus*, 767, 1995.

Pasca, V., 'Ross Lovegrove: una sensuale organicità', *D.E. Driade Edizioni*, 4, April 1997.

Zaera, A., 'Finding freedoms: Conversation with Rem Koolhaas', *El Croquis*, 1992, 53.

Zaera, A., 'fdidsasca', *El Croquis*, 1994, 65–66.

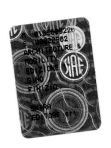